THE WORLD OF...

Geography
Revision

Andy Browne

Contents

Who would live in a place like this?

We orbited the planet for what one of its inhabitants would call a year. Our initial findings are that Earth, as it is known, would be unsuitable for colonisation by our people.

The planet appears to be cracking up. This is not something that has happened overnight. The outer surface of the planet, known as the <u>crust</u>, broke up and split as the planet cooled when it was first formed over four billion years ago.

COMMUNICATION: #@!‰¥œ≤156839/883/Z…
PLANET: #≤ã≠68973/YH2
Diameter: 12 756 km
Mass: 5 976 billion billion tonnes
Age: 4.6 billion years
Atmosphere: 78% Nitrogen, 21% Oxygen
Land surface: 150 million km^2
Intelligent life: Doubtful

The surface of the planet is made up of great sections of crust, which float on a liquid version of the rock underneath, called <u>magma</u>. The crust is 6–40 km thick. The layer of magma is approximately 2900 km thick; this is named the <u>mantle</u>, where the molten rock is at an impressive temperature of 1500–3000 °C.

mantle
crust
outer core
inner core

The structure of the Earth

In addition, it is dangerous at the edges of these sections of crust, called <u>tectonic plates</u>. As they move against each other they rub, causing the ground to shake with disastrous consequences – quite literally an earthquake. In the worst cases, the plates become caught against each other and the forces pushing the plates build up, until they suddenly break free. The energy released is enough to tear down the fragile structures the people build, often resulting in great loss of life.

If this wasn't enough, along these edges, or <u>plate boundaries</u>, the liquid rock is liable to burst from deep underground and incinerate anything or anyone that comes into contact with it. Like the build up of forces from the earthquakes, sometimes the liquid rock, or <u>lava</u>, doesn't break out of the ground immediately. Pressure can build up and whole mountains, known as <u>volcanoes</u>, can explode.

Why anyone would chose to live on this planet I don't know. It seems to be extremely hazardous, with injury or death around every corner. I have not even started to mention the various diseases, wild creatures or Girls Aloud.

I don't think so!

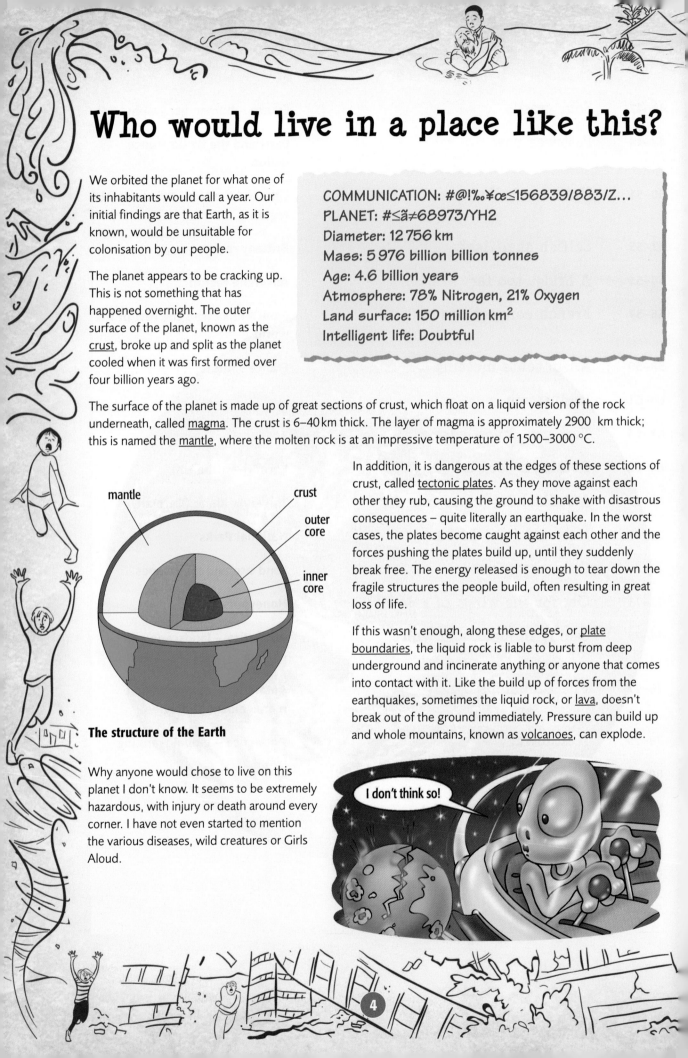

It is incredible to think that the surface of our planet is broken into massive sections and that the rock beneath it is so hot that it has stayed molten. However, the evidence of this is all around us, from the drama of volcanic eruptions and violent earthquakes, to the imperceptible drift of the continents over millions of years. This diagram shows the location of the Earth's plates and their boundaries.

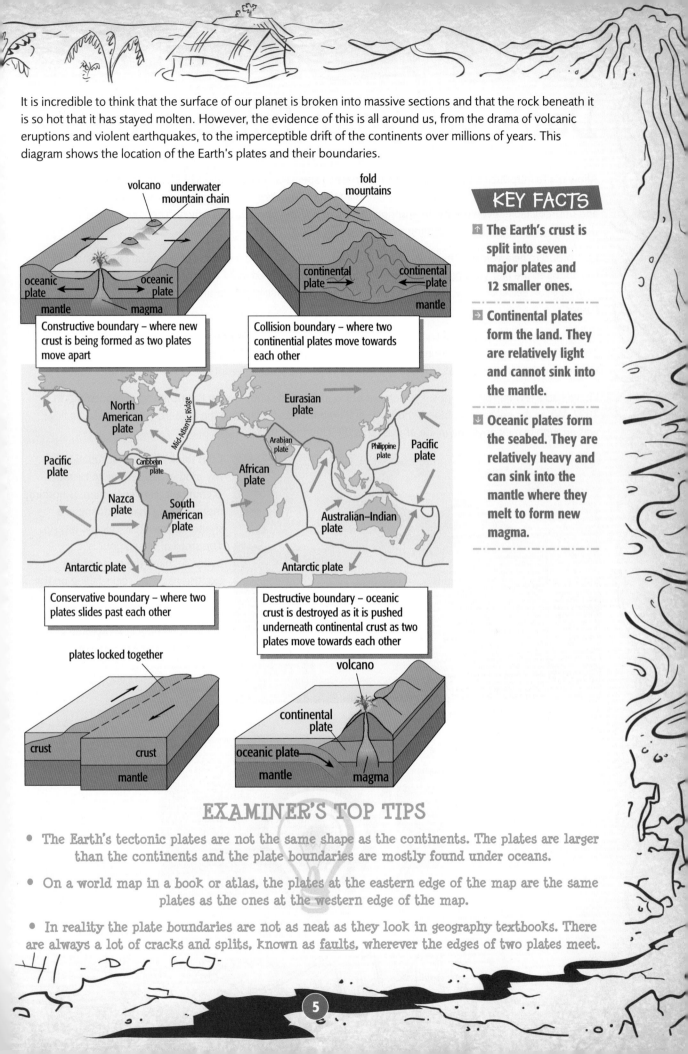

volcano underwater mountain chain

oceanic plate

oceanic plate

mantle   magma

Constructive boundary – where new crust is being formed as two plates move apart

fold mountains

continental plate

continental plate

mantle

Collision boundary – where two continential plates move towards each other

North American plate

Mid-Atlantic Ridge

Eurasian plate

Arabian plate

Philippine plate

Pacific plate

Pacific plate

Caribbean plate

African plate

Nazca plate

South American plate

Australian–Indian plate

Antarctic plate

Antarctic plate

Conservative boundary – where two plates slides past each other

Destructive boundary – oceanic crust is destroyed as it is pushed underneath continental crust as two plates move towards each other

plates locked together

crust

crust

mantle

volcano

continental plate

oceanic plate

mantle   magma

EXAMINER'S TOP TIPS

• The Earth's tectonic plates are not the same shape as the continents. The plates are larger than the continents and the plate boundaries are mostly found under oceans.

• On a world map in a book or atlas, the plates at the eastern edge of the map are the same plates as the ones at the western edge of the map.

• In reality the plate boundaries are not as neat as they look in geography textbooks. There are always a lot of cracks and splits, known as <u>faults</u>, wherever the edges of two plates meet.

Don't get your fingers burnt

Allow me to introduce myself. I am a volcano chaser. I specialise in collecting samples from <u>active volcanoes</u> and filming them. <u>Extinct</u> or <u>dormant</u> ones are of no interest to me. Volcanoes can be extremely violent, destructive and unpredictable. Even during an <u>eruption</u> there can be long periods of inactivity. Then, in a moment, you are dodging <u>volcanic bombs</u> and running from <u>pyroclastic flows</u>.

I am proud to be a volcano chaser. I believe that I am following in the footsteps of historical figures such as Pliny the Younger, the first <u>vulcanologist</u>. When Mount Vesuvius erupted in 79 AD, the Romans had no word in their language for 'volcano'. Pliny used phrases such as 'gusts of igneous serpentine vapour' and 'long fantastic flames'.

Today I have my own fireproof suit, which can withstand temperatures of up to 1200°C. I carry a GPS (global positioning system), satellite phone, laptop and digital video camera. I can keep in touch with the scientists monitoring the volcano as well as make recordings when the volcano erupts.

I have had a few narrow escapes. I remember being airlifted to safety on the Pacific island of Montserrat in 1997. When the volcano exploded, the town of Plymouth was buried and the heat from the pyroclastic flow was enough to melt anything made of glass that the cloud reached.

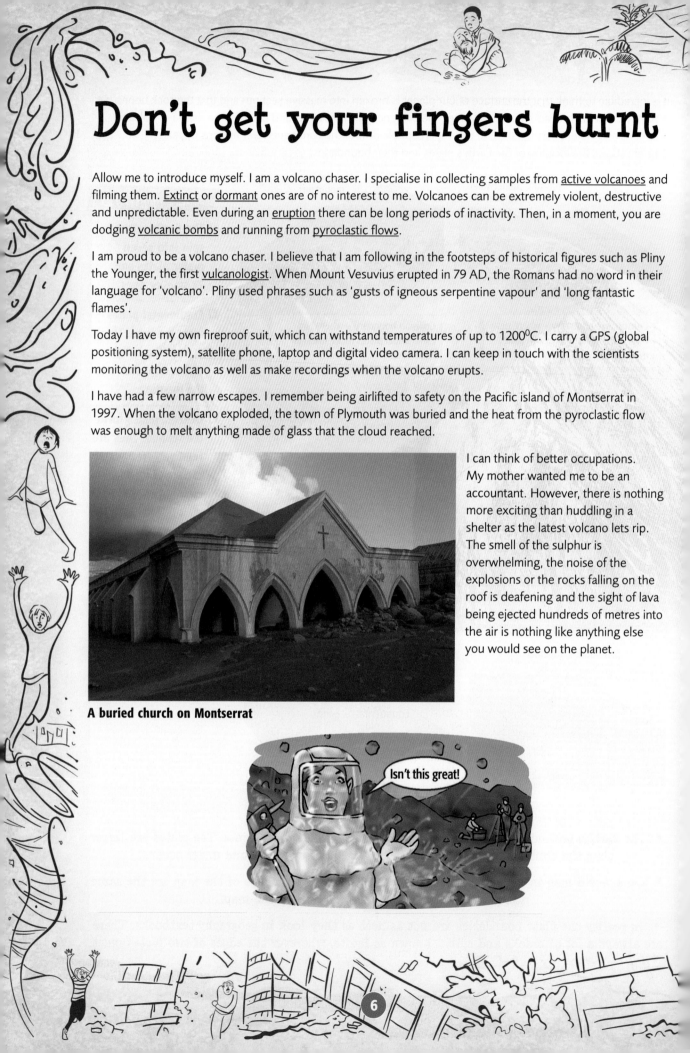

A buried church on Montserrat

I can think of better occupations. My mother wanted me to be an accountant. However, there is nothing more exciting than huddling in a shelter as the latest volcano lets rip. The smell of the sulphur is overwhelming, the noise of the explosions or the rocks falling on the roof is deafening and the sight of lava being ejected hundreds of metres into the air is nothing like anything else you would see on the planet.

⬆ There are approximately 1500 active volcanoes in the world today.

➡ Volcanic bombs are red hot boulders ejected from the volcano. Some can be the size of a bungalow.

⬇ Pyroclastic flows are suffocating clouds of ash and dust at temperatures of 1000⁰C that travel down the sides of volcanoes at speeds of 100–200 km/hour.

A volcanic landscape

⬇ Lahars are rivers of volcanic ash mixed with surface water, they are virtually unstoppable and extremely destructive.

⬅ There are two main types of volcano:

- Composite or Strato volcanoes, these are steep sided and cone shaped. They are made from layers of thick, sticky lava and ash. They are usually found at destructive plate boundaries. Composite volcanoes have the most explosive eruptions.

- Shield volcanoes, are flat and wide. They are made from thin, runny lava and are usually found at constructive plate boundaries. Shield volcanoes tend to have gentle eruptions, when lava flows quickly over the ground.

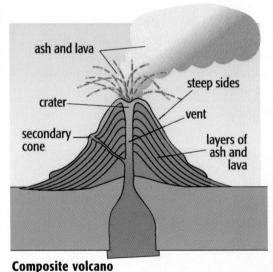

Composite volcano

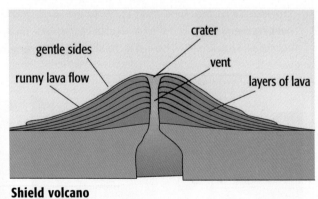

Shield volcano

EXAMINER'S TOP TIP

If you are asked to write about a volcanic eruption in an exam, make sure that you can describe and explain the movements of the Earth's plates that caused the volcano, as well as the changes that happened to the volcano itself that led up to the eruption.

Fire walking

Date: 18th January, 2002.

Yesterday my school burnt down. It wasn't the act of an unhappy pupil, or a teacher wanting an extra holiday. My school was destroyed by a river of lava that flowed through the town.

My name is Joseph Ogumu and I am 13 years old. I live with my parents and three younger sisters in Goma, a town that until yesterday had a population of about half a million people.

We live on the edge of a beautiful lake called Kivu, surrounded by eight mountains. I like to go walking and climbing in the mountains at weekends, but you do have to watch out as they are all volcanoes – and you can meet the occasional gorilla.

The most active volcano near us is Mount Nyiragongo. It is 3496 metres (11380 feet) high and only 10 km (6 miles) from the town. The last time it erupted was in 1996.

Yesterday the volcano erupted again. The lava has completely destroyed a 50 metre-wide strip of houses, shops, roads and schools right through Goma. It is as if someone has taken an enormous rubber and just dragged it across the town. There have been massive explosions where petrol stations and factories have been touched by the lava.

The lava flow looks like the surface of the Moon. In some places it is too hot to walk on; in other places people have dug holes into it to cook meals using the heat from the still molten rock below.

We are going to need a huge amount of aid from the rest of the world to get us back to normal. 300 000 people have fled the town. They have nowhere to go and many have no house or job to go back to. We were a relatively poor town by world standards in the first place. Now we are going to need help more than ever. We will need emergency food and water supplies to start with, as well as shelter and medical facilities. Then the task of rebuilding can begin.

High Street, Goma, 2002

Goma is in the Democratic Republic of Congo, right on the border with Rwanda, in Central Africa. The impact of a volcanic eruption in a Less Economically Developed Country (LEDC) may be far worse than in a More Economically Developed Country (MEDC). LEDC's may not have the same resources as MEDC's to predict or respond to eruptions. Damage to property and loss of life can be far higher than it should be and it can take a lot longer for life to return to normal for the communities affected.

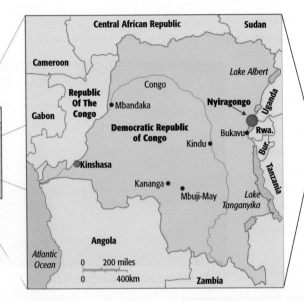

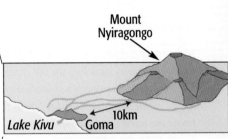

The location of Mount Nyiragongo

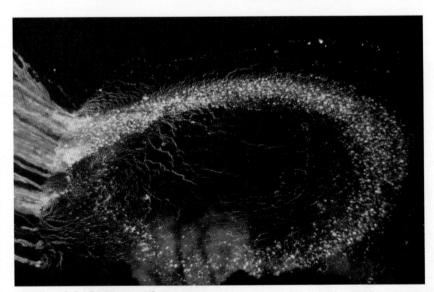

The lava lake in Mount Niragongo

KEY FACTS

→ Mount Nyiragongo has a lava lake that sometimes appears in its crater just before it erupts. In 2002 the lake was 40 metres across.

EXAMINER'S TOP TIP

The effect of the eruption on Goma was not as catastrophic as it could have been. The lava was thin and runny so there were no pyroclastic flows or volcanic bombs. This type of lava is known as <u>basic</u> or <u>basaltic lava</u>.

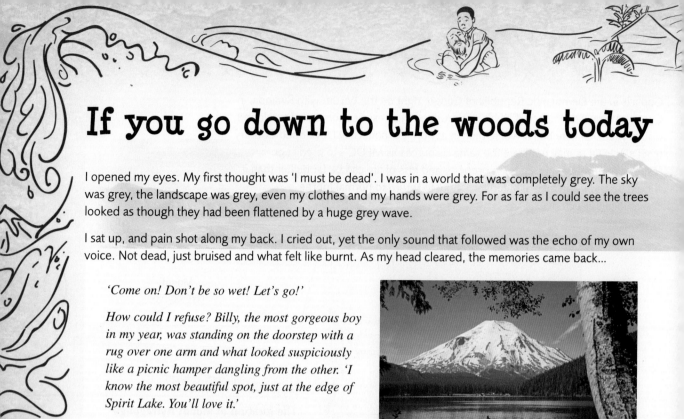

If you go down to the woods today

I opened my eyes. My first thought was 'I must be dead'. I was in a world that was completely grey. The sky was grey, the landscape was grey, even my clothes and my hands were grey. For as far as I could see the trees looked as though they had been flattened by a huge grey wave.

I sat up, and pain shot along my back. I cried out, yet the only sound that followed was the echo of my own voice. Not dead, just bruised and what felt like burnt. As my head cleared, the memories came back...

'Come on! Don't be so wet! Let's go!'

How could I refuse? Billy, the most gorgeous boy in my year, was standing on the doorstep with a rug over one arm and what looked suspiciously like a picnic hamper dangling from the other. 'I know the most beautiful spot, just at the edge of Spirit Lake. You'll love it.'

'Are you out of your mind?!', I replied. 'That's right in the middle of the <u>exclusion zone</u>. You know that no one is allowed within 20km of the mountain. It's been rumbling for weeks, that bulge on the North side has been getting larger and larger, and the <u>vulcanologists</u> say it could blow at any minute.'

Mt St Helens before its erruption

'Rubbish!', he said. 'It could be weeks, if not years before anything happens. This is a once in a lifetime offer. Anyway, if she does blow, I'll be there to protect you...'

Mt St Helens after its erruption

Cautiously, I got to my feet. Volcanic ash cascaded from me. It was a miracle that I had survived.

I knew all about Mt St Helens. Its eruptions in the past had been incredibly violent. There was evidence to show that <u>pyroclastic flows</u> had once rushed down the side of the volcano. With a record like that, only a fool would have gone for a picnic at the foot of the mountain. Wearily I began to make my way through the devastated forest towards my family. Looking back I could see no trace of the rug, picnic... or Billy.

Mt St Helens is on the West coast of the USA. The volcano is caused by the Juan de Fuca plate being pushed underneath the North American Plate. The Juan de Fuca plate melts, increasing the amount of molten rock in the mantle, so the rock is forced upwards into the Cascade Mountains.

Mt St Helen's is a <u>composite volcano</u>. It is made from lava with a high silica content, which makes it sticky. This type of lava solidifies as it reaches the ground surface forming a plug, a bit like a cork, which stops the lava underneath from escaping. Pressure builds up until eventually the volcano explodes, with catastrophic consequences.

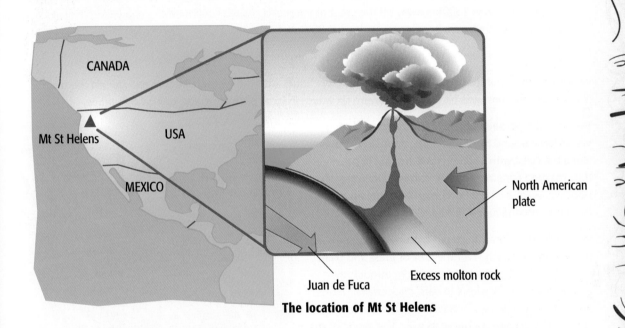

The location of Mt St Helens

KEY FACTS

➡ **The volcano erupted on May 18 1980, it had been dormant for over 120 years.**

➡ **The eruption killed 61 people, lowered the height of the summit of Mt St Helens by 390 metres and flattened over ten million trees.**

⬆ **The plug at Mt St Helens forced the lava to build up on the north side of the volcano. This created a bulge called a <u>cryptodome</u>, and this is why the volcano erupted sideways, rather than upwards.**

EXAMINER'S TOP TIP

Aim to make links or connections in your answers. You could try linking different parts of the same issue, such as how the type of lava found at Mt St Helens led to the eruption happening sideways. You could also make links between the eruption at Mt St Helens and other eruptions, such as those at Montserrat and Goma; how and why are they similar and different?

Waves of destruction

Every year we go on holiday at Christmas. In 2004 my parents chose Sri Lanka because of its reputation for calm seas and gorgeous weather. Our hotel was on the south west coast.

Christmas Day began with a swim and then church with the locals in the nearby village. On our return we made the most of the festivities the hotel had laid on. Turkey with all the trimmings, presents, carol singing and a party that went on late into the night.

I woke in the night with a deep sense of unease and found that Mum and Dad had woken too. We couldn't work out what had roused us, so we went back to sleep. We learnt later that we must have felt the earthquake that had just happened 1600 km away off the coast of Indonesia. As we continued to sleep we were oblivious to the <u>tsunami</u> waves that were heading towards us at 800 km/h.

On Boxing Day we relaxed in our room instead of going to the beach. That probably saved our lives.

There was no warning when the waves hit, about two hours after the earthquake that had caused them. Sri Lanka's east coast was hit first – there were six waves in total, each weighing 100 billion tonnes.

We should have been safe on the west coast, but the waves bent around the island and continued to travel along the coast with unpredictable results. In places they reached 6 metres high. A train running along the track that went past our hotel was lifted from its rails and flung into the jungle, killing all its passengers.

We watched in horror from our balcony as the sea poured up the beach, over the area of grass and palm trees at the front of the hotel, and then through the ground floor. It took with it towels, deck chairs, debris from the beach, and anyone who was unfortunate enough not to have got out of its way. The sound of the rushing water and the screams of the people below will stay with me for the rest of my life.

- The earthquake that caused the tsunami measured 9.3 on the <u>Richter scale</u>, the second most powerful earthquake ever recorded. (The most powerful was the Great Chilean earthquake in 1960 at 9.5 on the Richter scale, which killed 2230 people.)

- The earthquake lasted for about ten minutes.

- The <u>epicentre</u> was 240 km west of the Indonesian island of Sumatra.

- The fault line was 1200 km long.

- It happened at a destructive plate boundary between the Indo-Australian plate and the Eurasian plate.

KEY FACTS

⇨ It took about 30 minutes for the first wave to hit Indonesia, the waves then travelled on to Malaysia, Thailand, India, Sri Lanka and many other Indian Ocean countries.

⇨ Just under 300 000 people were killed by the tsunami.

⇦ 43 832 people were killed in Sri Lanka, the majority on the east coast of the island.

⇨ 126 000 people were killed in Indonesia. The greatest loss of life happened in Banda Aceh, a town on the tip of Sumatra, which was completely obliterated.

⇨ As a response, people in the UK donated £300 million to the Disasters Emergency Relief Fund.

Devastation caused by the tsunami

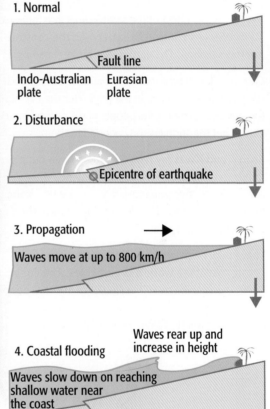

1. Normal

Indo-Australian plate   Eurasian plate   Fault line

2. Disturbance

Epicentre of earthquake

3. Propagation

Waves move at up to 800 km/h

4. Coastal flooding

Waves rear up and increase in height

Waves slow down on reaching shallow water near the coast

The epicentre of the earthquake

Bangladesh
India   Burma
Thailand
Somalia   Andaman and Nicobar Islands   Malaysia
Sri Lanka   Maldives
Kenya
Seychelles
Tanzania   Indonesia

EXAMINER'S TOP TIPS

• Tsunami waves can be formed by landslides as well as earthquakes.

• In the ocean, the waves may be less than one metre high. The waves 'rear up' as they reach the coast because friction slows the water at the bottom of the wave, while the water at the top of the wave continues to travel towards land at high speed.

• In Indonesia and Thailand the sea appeared to 'draw back' before the wave hit, but in Sri Lanka there were no warning signs. This is because the waves hit Indonesia and Thailand trough first, whereas they hit Sri Lanka peak first.

Shaken not stirred?

It was my job to protect the city from the effects of an earthquake. My wife laughed at me. 'What sort of a job is it coordinating earthquake planning when there has been no <u>seismic</u> activity here for over 20 years?', she said. She didn't understand the honour or responsibility of managing the safety of the 1.5 million inhabitants of Kobe, Japan's fifth largest city.

The earthquake struck on the 17th January 1995 at 5.46 am. It began with a sharp jolt upwards, followed by violent shaking side to side. I never made it in to the office. The earthquake measured 7.6 on the Richter scale, enough to tear the city apart. The motorways collapsed, rail lines buckled and road surfaces were split.

Over 5000 people were killed, many by the <u>primary effect</u> of buildings collapsing on top of them. Others died in the <u>secondary effect</u> of the terrible fires that followed the quake. The earthquake ruptured gas mains, which burst into flame. I had personally supervised the construction of an emergency water pipe network across the city, for just this situation. The earthquake broke those pipes too, and the people had no water to put the fires out.

Over a million households lost water, electricity and telephone connections. In the days after the earthquake there was nothing for the people to eat or drink, and no way to get the supplies they needed to them.

People said it was my fault – I should have put more things in place. But how do you convince the authorities to give you more resources when Kobe was believed to be one of the least likely cities in the country to have a quake?

I have now been promoted to do the same job in Tokyo, one of the world's largest cities. The Great Kanto earthquake of 1923 killed over 100 000 people there. The seismologists predict that such an earthquake will hit Tokyo every 72.5 years so it is now well overdue.

Kobe after the earthquake

⊡ Japan is found at the junction of four of the earth's <u>tectonic plates</u>.

⊡ Japan experiences an average of 1000 earthquakes a year.

⊡ 35 000 people in Kobe were injured and 100 000 people were made homeless.

⊡ Japan has earthquake drills on the first of September every year, but when the earthquake hit Kobe, the people didn't have time to put what they had learnt into practice.

⊡ The city couldn't cope with the scale of the destruction. Ambulances and fire engines were unable to travel down the damaged roads. There was not enough emergency equipment like breathing apparatus and heat imaging cameras; hospitals couldn't treat all the casualties.

⊡ It took four days for the first sniffer dog to arrive to begin to search for anyone who was trapped.

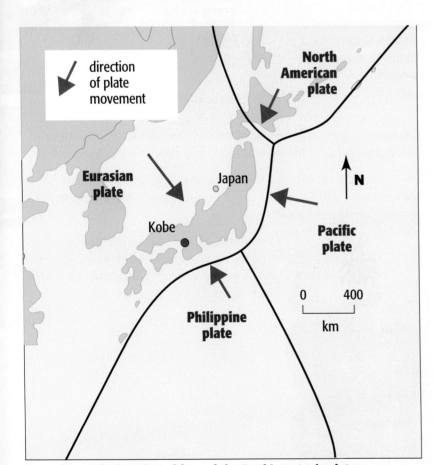

Japan lies at the junction of four of the Earth's tectonic plates

EXAMINER'S TOP TIP

Make the distinction between primary and secondary effects. Primary effects are caused as a direct result of an earthquake, such as buildings collapsing. Secondary effects are not directly caused by the earthquake, even if they are a consequence of the earthquake. Fire damage is a good example of a secondary effect.

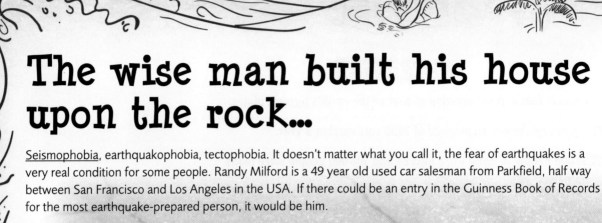

The wise man built his house upon the rock...

<u>Seismophobia</u>, earthquakophobia, tectophobia. It doesn't matter what you call it, the fear of earthquakes is a very real condition for some people. Randy Milford is a 49 year old used car salesman from Parkfield, half way between San Francisco and Los Angeles in the USA. If there could be an entry in the Guinness Book of Records for the most earthquake-prepared person, it would be him.

His house sits on rubber foundations sunk deep into the ground to reach the rocks below. The house is made from steel-framed concrete, which means it will twist and not collapse if an earthquake occurs.

Randy has painted the house with earthquake-proof paint, imported from Japan. The paint contains a type of plastic that strengthens the outer surfaces of a building. Inside his house Randy has installed a sprinkler system and there is a smoke alarm in every room.

The garden looks like a scene from a science fiction film. The lawn is covered in <u>tilt meters</u>, <u>creep meters</u>, <u>gravity meters</u>, <u>strain gauges</u> and laser measuring devices. Underground, in each corner of the garden, are Randy's four <u>seismometers</u>. These are all linked to a powerful computer, which not only acts as a warning device, but can tell Randy if he has any visitors and what size shoes they are wearing.

San Francisco
The San Andreas Fault, a few kilometers from Los Angeles. The reason why Randy is so nervous about a possible earthquake.

North American Plate
Moving north-westwards by 1 cm per year.

San Andreas Fault

N

USA

Pacific Plate
Moving north-westwards by 6 cm per year.

Los Angeles

San Diego

The San Andreas Fault

If all the technology fails, Randy has two cats, a dog and a pond full of Koi Carp. He applied for a licence to keep a giant panda in his shed, but it was turned down on the grounds that they were an endangered species.

Friends and family have told Randy that, despite all his efforts, it may not be enough to save his life if an earthquake were to happen. They are notoriously difficult to predict and any warning that might be given probably wouldn't allow him enough time to evacuate to a safe place.

Randy doesn't care and just tells everyone that one day his precautions will save him. Anyway, he's too busy attempting to conquer his other fear... spiders.

➡ Famous sufferers of earthquakophobia include Michael Jackson and Michael Stipe (lead singer of REM).

➡ Ancient Romans relied on earthenware jars containing stones as early warning systems. When the ground shook the stones fell from the mouths of dragons sculpted onto the jars, warning the jar's owner of the earthquake.

➡ Modern tower blocks employ many of the ideas contained in Randy's story. Some buildings also have counter-weights on the roof, which move in the opposite direction to the force of the earthquake.

➡ When people are killed by earthquakes, it is usually as the result of being squashed or hit by debris, not from being shaken.

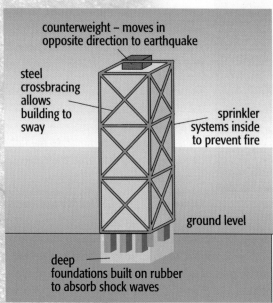

counterweight – moves in opposite direction to earthquake

steel crossbracing allows building to sway

sprinkler systems inside to prevent fire

ground level

deep foundations built on rubber to absorb shock waves

An earthquake proof building

EXAMINER'S TOP TIPS

• It is impossible to prevent earthquakes. However, the effect of earthquakes can be reduced by designing earthquake-proof buildings, predicting accurately when earthquakes are going to happen and having plans in place for when an earthquake does happen.

• One method of preventing earthquakes that has been tried is pumping water into faults. The idea is that this will allow the sections of the earth's crust to slide past each other more easily. In reality scientists think that this method is more likely to cause earthquakes than prevent them!

When the 'Fat Lady' sings

I am an old man and I want to enjoy my retirement in peace. I dream of days spent with my feet up on the veranda of my little house in Nicolosi overlooking the orange groves and vineyards, a glass of wine in one hand, a good book in the other.

But I am cursed. I am the man who first built the cable car that reaches far up the slopes of Mt Etna. After a lifetime of repairing and rebuilding kilometres of wires and support towers, it is me they call on whenever the 'Fat Lady' decides to sing.

I built the cable car system as a young man working for my father's company. That was in 1958. It was completely destroyed in 1971 by a lava flow. I had taken over the company by then, and it was my decision to rebuild it lower down the mountain to prevent the same thing happening again. But it did – everything was destroyed in 1983.

The Etna Cable car station during an eruption

When we had just about completed the repairs, another eruption in 1985 destroyed it. All was fine until 2001, when three support towers were wrecked by lava. They were rebuilt, only to be knocked down again two years later. It was then that I decided enough was enough, and I retired.

Some people might say building a cable car on the slopes of an <u>active volcano</u> was a ridiculous thing to do in the first place. 4000 tourists use it every day in the summer, so my father's decision to go ahead with the cable car has been proved right.

Other people argue that we are irresponsible to encourage tourists to visit such a dangerous location. However, in the last 100 years only 18 people have been killed by the mountain. It is one of the most closely monitored volcanoes in the world, so the authorities know when to keep people away. Also, the lava that Mt Etna produces is sticky and slow moving, so there is usually plenty of time to get out of the way.
I am proud of my contribution to the success of Mt Etna as a tourist attraction. For us, it's not over when the Fat Lady sings – it has only just begun.

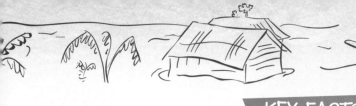

→ **Mt Etna is Europe's most active volcano. It is located on the Italian island of Sicily.**

→ **Scientists estimate that Mt Etna has been erupting for about 300 000 years. The earliest recorded eruption was in 475 B.C. and there have been at least 190 eruptions since then.**

↓ **Mt Etna is called the Fat Lady because of its size and character. It is approximately 3340 m high (it changes from year to year due to the volcanic activity) and 150 km around the base. That's an area of 1190km².**

The creation of Mt Etna

↑ **Well over 300 businesses depend on tourism around Mt Etna. The cable car is a crucial part of attracting the visitors to the volcano.**

← **When Mt Etna erupted for 24 days in a row in July and August 2001, the Italian government provided an aid package to tourist and agricultural businesses worth £5.6 million. That gives an indication of how important the volcano is to the local economy.**

→ **Nine tourists tragically lost their lives when Mt Etna exploded unexpectedly in 1979.**

↓ **The Italian authorities have used a number of strategies to prevent flows of lava from damaging settlements. These have included building diversion canals, spraying the lava with water and blowing it up using dynamite.**

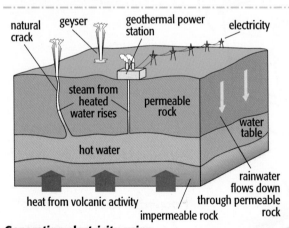

Generating electricity using geothermal energy

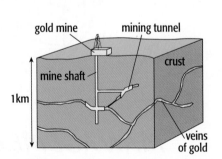

Mining for minerals deposited by volcanic activity

The structure of the earth is the inner core, outer core, mantle and crust.

The two types of plate are oceanic and continental.

CAUSES

There are four main types of plate boundary: constructive, destructive, collision and conservative.

Most volcanoes are found at constructive and destructive plate boundaries.

Earthquakes are found at any plate boundary.

VOLCAN AND EARTHQU

Tsunami warning systems for the Indian Ocean are being developed.

Earthquake-proof buildings can be built with rubber foundations, cross-bracing, counter-weights and flexibility.

MANAGEMENT

Earthquake drills are held every year in Japan.

KEEP OUT

Vulcanologists are able to predict the likelihood of an eruption in order to evacuate people.

Fish, animals, tilt meters, lasers and seismometers can all be used to predict earthquake activity.

Earthquakes are measured using the Richter scale.

Richter Scale
8,9
8
7
6
5
4
3
2
1
0

The Asian Tsunami killed almost 300,000 people on 26 December 2004.

Mt Nyiragongo destroyed Goma and 74 villages leaving 20,000 homeless on 17 January 2002.

CONSEQUENCES

The Kobe earthquake on 17 January 1995 killed 5000 people, injured 35,000 and left 100,000 homeless.

JES

AKES

Mt St Helens killed 67 people on 18 May 1980.

Mt Etna receives 4000 tourists a year.

FOR SALE

300 businesses around Mt Etna rely on tourism.

BENEFITS

Geothermal energy is used to generate electricity.

Farms near volcanoes use the fertile soil from eruptions.

Volcanoes release valuable minerals during eruptions.

Test your knowledge 1

1 Label the diagram of the structure of the earth using these labels:

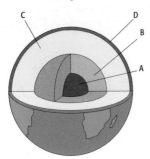

Inner core   Mantle
Outer core   Crust

(4 marks)

2 Name this plate from its outline.

(1 mark)

3 Identify each type of plate boundary from the diagrams below.

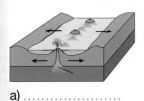 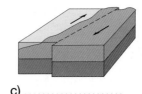 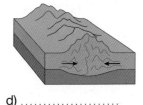

a) ....   b) ....   c) ....   d) ....

(4 marks)

4 Match the volcano with the correct labels.

Mt Etna or Mauna Loa?

- Composite
- Runny lava
- Gentle eruption
- Shield
- Sticky lava
- Pyroclastic flows

(6 marks)

5 Describe a pyroclastic flow in as much detail you can.

(4 marks)

6 Fill in the blanks from the paragraph below to explain why Mt St Helens erupted on the 18th May 1980. Choose from the words given beneath the paragraph.

The Juan de Fuca plate was moving towards the North American plate at a rate of a few .... a year. The .... plate was being pushed under the .... plate because it was an oceanic plate, which made it the heavier of the two plates. As the Juan de Fuca plate was being pushed into the ...., it melted and extra .... was produced. The molten rock was thick and sticky because it was mixed with .... from the Pacific Ocean. This extra molten rock increased the .... underground, so it pushed to the surface. Once inside Mt St Helens the path of the lava was blocked by .... from previous eruptions. Eventually the pressure inside the volcano became so great that the mountain literally ....

solidified lava	magma	North American	sediments
mantle	exploded	Juan de Fuca	millimetres	pressure

(9 marks)

7 Describe the effects of the Asian tsunami on Sri Lanka.

(5 marks)

8 What caused the Asian tsunami to happen? Put these statements in the correct order.

- The Indo-Australian plate was moving underneath the Eurasian plate.

- As the waves reached the coast, the bottom of the wave was slowed by friction, while the top of the wave continued to travel at high speed.

- The waves had such long wave lengths that they did not break when they hit the shore, and continued to flow inland for several miles.

- The shockwave caused by the earthquake sent waves travelling away from the fault at speeds of 500 km/hour.

- Pressure built up along the fault line between the two plates.

- The front of the wave reared up, then came crashing down onto the coast.

- The pressure was released when the Eurasian plate 'flicked' upwards.

(7 marks)

9 Why are the impacts of an earthquake or volcano usually worse for an LEDC than an MEDC?

(5 marks)

10 Why do people choose to live in places where there is a risk of earthquakes or volcanic eruptions?

(5 marks)

(Total 50 marks)

Living the high life?

My name is Kofi. I am 13 years old and I live in Malawi, in South East Africa. My home town is Chitimba, on the west coast of Lake Malawi.

I don't go to school. I would like to go to college to train to be a mechanic, but it is expensive so I am working hard to save enough for the course fees. I make my money from the tourists who pass through Chitimba on their way north or south along our M1. Eventually the government says they will tarmac all of it, as it is our most important road.

I take the tourists up a steep road into the mountains, to a village called Livingstonia. It's named after the famous explorer David Livingstone who was born in 1813. It was built by Scottish Missionaries over 100 years ago. British tourists say that it is just like going to Scotland, with a stone-built church, high street, hotel and post office. I've never been to Scotland, so I don't know if they are telling the truth.

The tourists give me money for showing them around. I take them to the Manchewe Falls, a spectacular waterfall 50 metres high. I show them the cave behind the falls where villagers used to hide from slave traders 100 years ago. I earn extra money by doing some washing for the tourists or mending their clothes.

It's not the sort of work that I imagined I'd be doing when I left primary school, but it will not be long before I can earn enough to begin my college course. It's hard to get work in Malawi, particularly a job that is well paid. However, if you are prepared to work hard, and make the most of your talents, you have the chance of doing well.

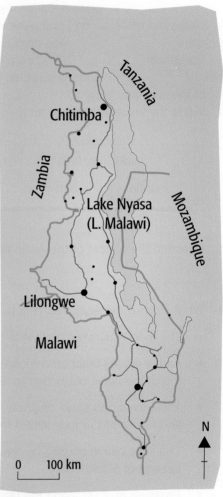

Malawi

Not everyone in Malawi lives in poverty. Some people have a quality of life and standard of living that is equal to the most well off in the UK. But most people are poor and the country is economically underdeveloped.

The causes of underdevelopment are complicated. The physical environment has an effect; Malawi suffers regularly from drought and the country has few natural resources. However, this isn't the whole answer.

Human factors are as important:

- For 30 years after independence Malawi was governed by a dictator, Hastings Kamuzu Banda. He is thought to have caused the disappearance of over 250 000 people.

- Malawi has large debts to the World Bank and the International Monetary Fund (IMF). Paying these debts means that Malawi has less money to spend on development.

- Malawi relies on agricultural products to earn money from other countries, and world prices for tobacco, sugar and tea have fallen recently.

KEY FACTS

➡ **Malawi was a British <u>colony</u> for 75 years, gaining its <u>independence</u> in 1964.**

➡ **Malawi is one of the least developed countries in the world. It is 13th from bottom out of the 177 countries included in the United Nations' <u>Human Development Index (HDI)</u>; the UK is 12th from the top.**

⬇ **The average life expectancy in Malawi is only 38 years old; in the UK it is 79.**

⬆ **<u>Gross Domestic Product (GDP)</u> per person is £322; in the UK it is £14 780.**

⬅ **85% of the people work in agriculture. They are either <u>subsistence</u> farmers (growing maize, millet and rice) or work on <u>commercial</u> plantations (growing tobacco, sugar and tea).**

➡ **Very few people work in manufacturing or <u>services</u>. Most of the jobs in these sectors are still connected to farming in some way such as selling or transporting food products.**

⬇ **Malawi's main <u>exports</u> are tobacco (76% of Malawi's export earnings), sugar and tea (20%).**

⬆ **<u>Adult literacy</u> in Malawi is 60%; in the UK it is 99%.**

⬅ **Malawi receives £251.5 million a year in <u>aid</u>; the UK gives £2.5 billion to the developing world.**

EXAMINER'S TOP TIPS

Beware of over-generalisation - making sweeping statements that are not necessarily true. For example, 'Everyone in Malawi is poor.' or 'Malawi is poor because the people are not as educated as us.'

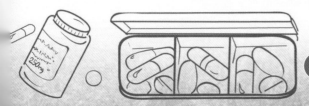

On top of the world

It was the 55th Miss World contest and floor manager John Craddock was sweating. The cause of his perspiration was not the heat of the Mexican evening, nor was it because he was the only man in a room of 177 beautiful women. The source of his discomfort was the argument that was rapidly spreading.

Miss Norway had started it. 'Norway is the best country', she boasted, 'because it has come top of the <u>United Nations'</u> rank of the <u>Human Development Index (HDI)</u>. It has scored highly in life expectancy, <u>adult literacy</u>, school enrolment and <u>Gross Domestic Product (GDP)</u>; giving it a top score of 0.956!'

This launched a row between the girls from the remaining countries in the top ten of the HDI. Miss Sweden, Miss Australia, Miss Iceland, Miss Japan and Miss Canada argued that people lived longer in their countries than in Norway. Miss Netherlands and Miss Belgium pointed out that their young people were better educated than Norway's. Miss Ireland explained that her country's GDP was practically identical to Norway's, and who had won the most Eurovision song contests anyway?!

Miss Austria began to claim that her country was best. It was the world's safest place to live, with less than one murder per million people a year.

'What about the environment?!', clamoured Miss Denmark. 'How can America, Canada or Japan claim to be great places to live when they are in the top ten list of countries most responsible for global warming?'

'Calm down all of you,' smiled Miss Venezuela. 'Did you know that in a recent survey my country contained the highest proportion of people who are happy? In spite of being 68th in the HDI?'

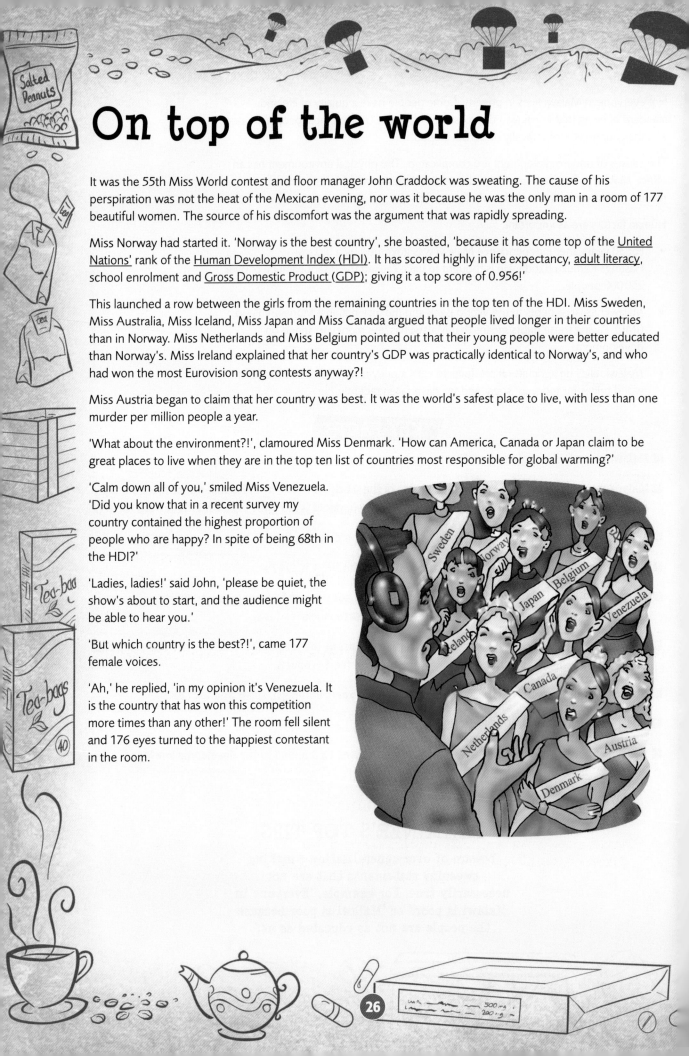

'Ladies, ladies!' said John, 'please be quiet, the show's about to start, and the audience might be able to hear you.'

'But which country is the best?!', came 177 female voices.

'Ah,' he replied, 'in my opinion it's Venezuela. It is the country that has won this competition more times than any other!' The room fell silent and 176 eyes turned to the happiest contestant in the room.

⤓ The HDI is one of the most useful measures of development because it is calculated using a combination of economic and social factors.

⇥ The best development indicators are easy to measure and make it simple to compare different countries. This is why adult literacy is a much more useful measure of education than average SATs results, because not all countries take SAT exams.

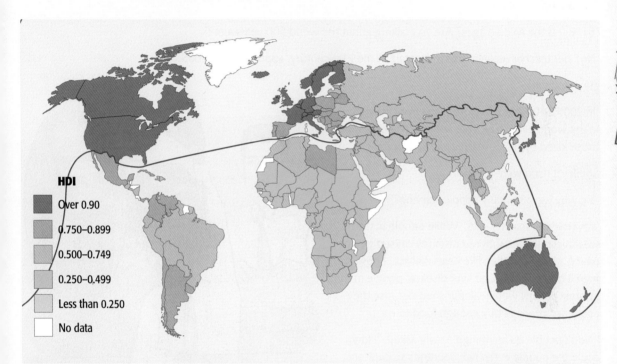

HDI

- Over 0.90
- 0.750–0.899
- 0.500–0.749
- 0.250–0.499
- Less than 0.250
- No data

Using measures of development it's possible to split the world into two halves: the rich north (MEDCs) and the poor south (LEDCs).

EXAMINER'S TOP TIPS

• Development indicators can be misleading. Usually they are an average figure, so they can hide inequalities within a country. For example, Saudi Arabia has one of the world's highest GDP per person, but the wealth is concentrated in the hands of a few very wealthy oil producers.

• Development is not just about economic growth and wealth. Education, health, the environment, freedom and justice are just as important.

Back to the future?

It is 2105, approximately 100 years from now. The scene is a Year 9 history classroom. Shelley is uncomfortable; she can't help being drawn in by her teacher's words...

'...800 million people were chronically hungry, 300 million of those were children... One child was dying every five seconds because they were too weak from hunger to fight common diseases... Seventeen million babies were being born every year underweight and <u>malnourished</u>...'

She put up her hand.

'Sir, is this the Middle ages? Are you talking about the world 500 years ago?'

'No,' her teacher replied, 'this is the start of the 21st century, approximately 2005.'

He continued.

'In 2005 24 000 people were dying from starvation in the world every day. That was more people than those killed by AIDS, malaria and TB combined.'

Shelley's hand went up again.

'Sir, why were so many people starving?'

'Poverty,' her teacher said. 'While people in the wealthiest nations suffered diseases caused by not eating a balanced diet, like heart disease, <u>obesity</u>, high blood pressure and liver disease, people in the poorest nations were malnourished because they could not afford to buy enough food to eat.'

'Didn't people do anything?' Shelly asked. 'How could the people in the rich countries sit back and allow this to happen? I'm sure everyone had television and the Internet by then.'

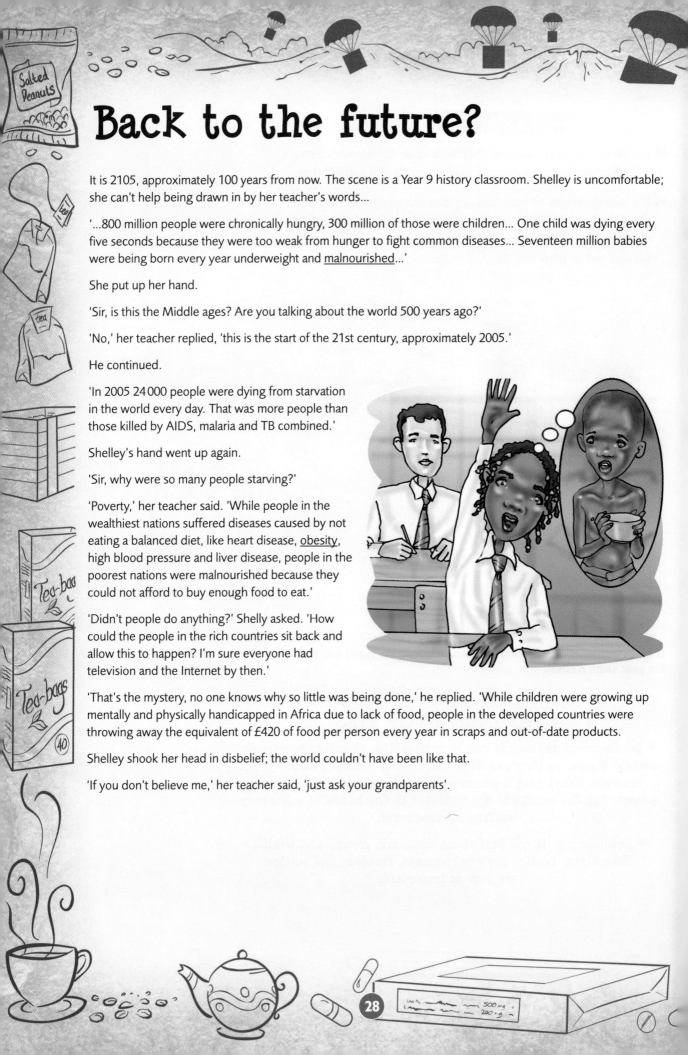

'That's the mystery, no one knows why so little was being done,' he replied. 'While children were growing up mentally and physically handicapped in Africa due to lack of food, people in the developed countries were throwing away the equivalent of £420 of food per person every year in scraps and out-of-date products.

Shelley shook her head in disbelief; the world couldn't have been like that.

'If you don't believe me,' her teacher said, 'just ask your grandparents'.

KEY FACTS

◄ The recommended daily intake of calories (calorific intake) is 2500 for men and 2000 for women.

► In some developed countries, the average intake is over 1000 more calories than are recommended. This is the reverse in some developing countries.

↓ The world produces more than enough food to feed everyone.

↑ Some farmers in developing countries do not own enough land to grow the food that they and their families need.

◄ Some developing countries grow <u>cash crops</u> on their best farmland. The plan is to sell the cash crops abroad and buy food out of the profits. However, if prices fall on the world market, this cannot happen.

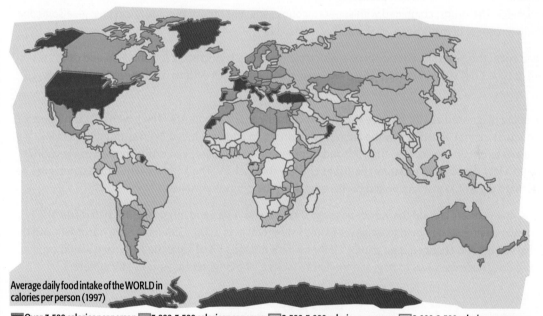

Average daily food intake of the WORLD in calories per person (1997)

■ Over 3,500 calories per person ■ 3,000-3,500 calories per person ■ 2,500-3,000 calories per person □ 2,000-2,500 calories per person
□ Under 2,000 calories per person ■ No available data

EXAMINER'S TOP TIP

Many students blame drought and wars for causing world hunger. A recent United Nations report calculated that it is only possible to account for 8% of global hunger by these factors. The other 92% is caused by economic factors.

Dying for a cure

Jeremy Mitchell was a happy man. For three years he had protested in front of the GlaxoSmithKline (GSK) UK headquarters in Brentford, West London. Finally his dream had come true. GSK had agreed to allow companies in Africa to manufacture its AIDS drugs at a cost far less than GSK would normally charge.

The GSK building in West London

It was an issue close to Jeremy's heart. He had been diagnosed as HIV positive in 2000. However, he knew that his prospects were very good. In the UK, being HIV positive is not necessarily a death sentence. This is due to powerful <u>antiretroviral</u> drugs. These drugs have the ability to limit the spread of the HIV virus in someone who has been infected and prevent it from leading to AIDS. The drugs, combined with support, counselling and regular medical checkups, give someone with HIV the prospect of many years of a relatively normal life.

Jeremy had spent the years since his diagnosis with a banner and a loudspeaker marching up and down the pavement outside GSK's brand new building. He knew that if he was an African, his future would be very different.

In Africa, being diagnosed as HIV positive was almost certainly a death sentence. The governments of most African countries cannot afford to buy the antiretroviral drugs. In addition, it had been a struggle for many African nations to obtain the licences they needed from American and European drugs companies like GSK, which would allow them to manufacture the drugs cheaply themselves. The argument the drugs companies had given was that they would lose out on the profits of making the drugs themselves.

Jeremy, and many others around the world, believed that this was unfair and inhumane. He had made his feelings known whenever he could to whoever would listen to him. In 2003, GSK must have heard him and the other global voices, and changed their minds. GSK now only charges 5% of what they normally would expect international drug manufacturers to pay, and the future looks a little brighter for Africa's HIV sufferers.

- If you were born in Zimbabwe last year, your average <u>life expectancy</u> would be about 33 years. The chances are that you would die from AIDS, which is now the main cause of death in Africa.

- If you were born in the UK last year, your average life expectancy would be 79 years. You would be likely to die of old age.

- In Africa it used to cost about £3392 a year to supply one person with enough drugs to hold back the spread of HIV. In some parts of Africa the average income is just £17 a month, so individuals had little hope of raising the money needed.

- The changes made by GSK mean that the cost of a year's supply of antiretroviral drugs in Africa has fallen to just £180 a year.

KEY FACTS

⬆ **In Zimbabwe 25% of the population is HIV positive.**

⬅ **In the UK less than 1% of the population is HIV positive – less than 54 000 people.**

➡ **Out of those people with HIV, roughly 800 a year will develop AIDS.**

⬇ **Each year there are about 5000 new cases of HIV diagnosed in the UK.**

⬆ **Since the 1980s there have been just over 13 000 deaths from AIDS in the UK.**

⬅ **28 million people in Africa are HIV positive.**

➡ **Each year there are about 3.4 million new cases of HIV diagnosed in Africa.**

⬇ **Every year, 2.3 million people die from AIDS in Africa – the equivalent of 6300 a day or an Asian tsunami every couple of months.**

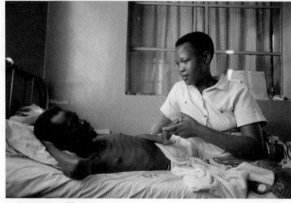

An AIDS sufferer

EXAMINER'S TOP TIPS

- Preventing deaths from AIDS is not just a matter of providing the appropriate drugs. Education about preventing infection from the HIV virus is vital.

- Uganda has moved from a situation of 18% of the population having HIV in 2000, to 6% of the population with HIV today.

- This has been the result of a government campaign. The ABC initiative promotes Abstinence (from sex before marriage), Being faithful (to just one partner) and using Condoms. This has been supported by $100 million of aid from the USA, including handing out 80 million free condoms a year.

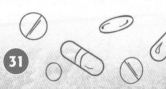

World trade is nuts!

Nadia sat in the doorway of her hut in Senegal, a small country on the west coast of Africa. She gazed out at her field of groundnut (peanut) plants. There was nowhere to hide from the heat of the sun. It was 40°C in the shade and the inside of her mud-walled home was like an oven. She was desperate for a drink, but she had no money to buy one.

She could sell her crop, but the plants were as parched as she was. Even if she could water them, she had nowhere to store the harvested nuts and no means to transport them to the local market. It was pointless, as there was no one to buy the nuts from her. People bought their nuts from abroad these days.

A peanut plant

Nadia could remember the good old days when the state peanut oil company SONACOS had been around. They had provided her with the money to buy seeds and tools, they had helped with watering and harvesting, they had bought groundnuts at a fair price, and they had collected them from her farm.

What had gone wrong?

Twenty years ago Senegal had been in trouble. Drought and a decline in the global economy had left the country with a large amount of debt. It desperately needed help to pay off the debts and continue to develop. The World Bank and the International Monetary Fund (IMF) had given Senegal a loan to help out. But the loan came with conditions: these were to concentrate on peanut farming, open up the country to world trade and encourage individual businesses.

The Senegalese government was forced to shut down SONACOS, so individual farmers had to fend for themselves. World trade resulted in the country being flooded with cheap foreign imports. Farmers like Nadia had found themselves with no market for their produce and no support from the government to help them with their farms.

Nadia shifted her position in the dust and a gust of wind rustled the dead leaves of her peanut plants. More rumours had come her way. World leaders had agreed to cancel 17% of the debt over the next ten years. She gave a wry smile; 17% of $3.5 billion was a drop in the ocean and, of course, this new initiative came with its own set of conditions.

In the UK we benefit from world trade in a number of ways:

- We have opportunities to buy food that we are not able to grow ourselves.

- We can buy seasonal products all year round.

- We pay low prices for our food.

LEDCs should also benefit from world trade:

- By concentrating on growing the crops that the LEDC grows best, maximum profits should be made. This money can then be used to help the country to develop.

- In reality, world trade is unfair; MEDCs benefit and LEDCs suffer.

KEY FACTS

- Debt is equal to 70% of Senegal's GDP.

- Debt is 200 times more than the money Senegal makes from its exports.

- 25% of Senegal's population is undernourished.

- 80% of the population earns less than £1.13 a day.

- The country spends more on debt repayments than it does on health and education combined.

- Senegal imports onions from Holland, tomatoes from Italy, rice from Thailand and peanuts from America, Argentina and Brazil.

The Ecoregions of Senegal

- West-Central Agricultural Region
- Agricultural Expansion Region
- Saloum Agricultural Region
- Northern Pastoral Sandy Region
- Ferrugineuse Pastoral Region
- Southern Pastoral Sandy Region
- Senegal River Valley
- Eastern Transition Region
- Shield Region
- Casamance
- Estuary Region
- Great Coast
- Dakar Region

EXAMINER'S TOP TIPS

Remember to give a balanced answer to questions. World trade has advantages as well as disadvantages.

Flying around the world

I checked my facts on my notepad as I bent my head backwards to look up at the largest passenger aeroplane in the world, the Airbus 380. Mere numbers couldn't prepare you for the awesome size of it.

However, I wasn't interested in technical details; my job was to attach the country of origin label. If you look in every book, on every toy, at each item of clothing or electronic equipment you own, you will always be able to find a country of origin label. Well, it's the same with aircraft, and it was my responsibility to do it for this one.

Length: 73 metres
Wing span: 79.8 metres
Height: 21.4 metres
Weight: 421 tonnes
Engines: 4
Number of wheels: 22
Passengers: 840
Speed: 0.85 x the speed of sound
Registration: F-WWOW

But I had a problem. The Airbus is manufactured by the European Aeronautic Defence and Space Company (EADS), which is joint-owned by four companies from France, Germany, Spain and the UK.

The Airbus 380 is assembled in Europe, and most of its major components are made in Europe. But the plane is actually put together from parts provided by 1500 suppliers around the world. The aircraft is a testament to the powers of globalisation.

The tyres are made by Michelin, a French company. However, the rubber comes from Michelin's own rubber plantations in Brazil and Nigeria. The bearings and rods used in the aircraft are made by Minebea Co. Ltd, a Japanese company, with factories in Japan, America and the UK. The wings and the engines are made in the UK, the tail is made in Spain and Germany, the fuselage is made in France and Germany and the nose is made in France.

Twenty-one companies that supply components are Japanese, 4% of the plane is made in Belgium and Airbus buys $80 million worth of parts a year from China.

I had to make a decision quickly. The Airbus 380 is due to start flying passengers in 2006. The company expects to make a total of 700, at a rate of about four new planes a month. Already virtually every major airline has ordered one. The United Arab Emirates has ordered 45!

I scratched my head and chewed the end of my biro, then it came to me in a flash! I returned to my office triumphant, safe in the knowledge that every 380 touching down on a runway would have a label attached to it saying... 'country of origin...please see arrivals board'.

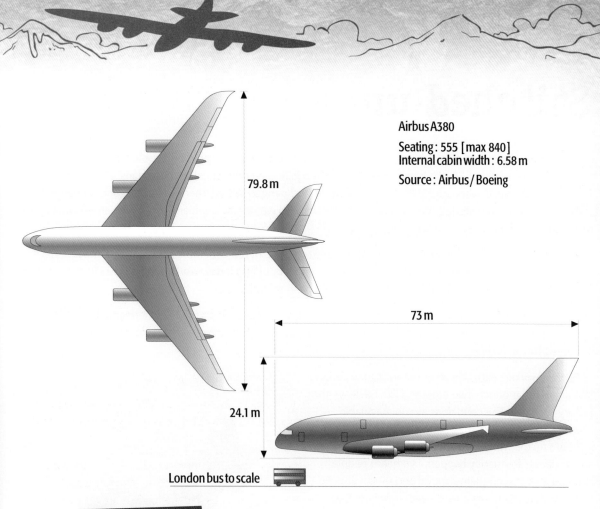

Airbus A380

Seating : 555 [max 840]
Internal cabin width : 6.58 m

Source : Airbus / Boeing

79.8 m

73 m

24.1 m

London bus to scale

KEY FACTS

⬇ You can fit 35 million ping-pong balls into an Airbus 380, or the equivalent of 10 squash courts.

➡ Each engine reaches a temperature equal to half the temperature on the surface of the Sun, and a pressure 50 times the Earth's atmospheric pressure.

⬇ EADS has employees from 85 different countries.

⬆ By 2016, one out of every five flights from Heathrow will be an Airbus 380.

⬅ No country produces everything that it needs by itself. Countries specialise in producing certain products and then exchange these with products from other countries.

EXAMINER'S TOP TIP

Globalisation is the spread of economic activity world wide. Due to the infinite number of connections between countries in the 21st century, every country is dependent on all the other countries. Make sure that you are able to include globalisation in any answer you give concerning world trade and economic development.

Stitched up

It's been a month since they picked me. Taken from my home country of Benin by people I'd never met before, I've entered a world that I didn't know existed. I've been joined by others; Italians, Germans, Namibians and Australians. We've all witnessed suffering, exploitation and danger. We've been twisted beyond recognition, stabbed, drowned and stoned. We've made it to the UK, and we're now on nearly every high street, waiting to be taken home for money.

My story begins on the south west coast of Africa, in Benin, one of the continent's poorest countries. Benin's climate is ideal for growing cotton. The cotton pickers earn about 60p a day, working long hours in the baking hot sun. Many of the pickers are children, who should be in school.

From Benin I travel to Italy, where my cotton is dyed using a synthetic indigo made in Germany. 17 000 tonnes of this dye is used each year. Its manufacture involves highly poisonous dioxins that pollute the environment. The dyed thread is then woven into denim, and sent to Tunisia.

African cotton

In Tunisia, workers earn 58p an hour turning my denim into a finished product. Two thousand like me leave the factory each day. The conditions are unimaginable. There are no safety guards on the machines, the pressure on the workers to keep up production is huge and accidents frequently happen. I've heard people shouted at, I've seen them slapped and their hair pulled. Some work for 80 hours a week, with only two days off a month. Still they don't earn enough to send their children to school, buy luxuries such as new clothes or books, or even afford to eat three healthy meals a day.

I'm stone-washed using pumice from a Turkish volcano. The landscape in Turkey is being destroyed as a result of pumice quarrying. Indigo released in the stone washing kills fish and plants in Tunisia.

My story ends 40 000 miles after it began, a few miles from your home. I lie, folded in a clothes shop, waiting to be picked up for about £30. It cost just £5 to make me, less than 1% of that going on the wages paid to the people who did all the hard work. It's not just me who's been stitched up.

KEY FACTS

⬇ The globalisation of the fashion industry has created this situation, where the components for a pair of jeans come from all over the world. At each stage of the production process people are being exploited and the environment is being damaged.

➡ The jeans' buttons come from Germany. They are made using copper from Namibia and zinc from Australia. The Namibian copper could be used to make ornaments and sold for more money than buttons. Arsenic, a highly toxic chemical is released as a by-product of the copper extraction process.

↙ Sweatshop conditions exist all round the world, but particularly in countries like Indonesia, Cambodia, China, Romania and Guatemala.

↗ There are about 100 deaths a year amongst cotton farmers in Benin due to the large amounts of pesticides that are sprayed onto the plants.

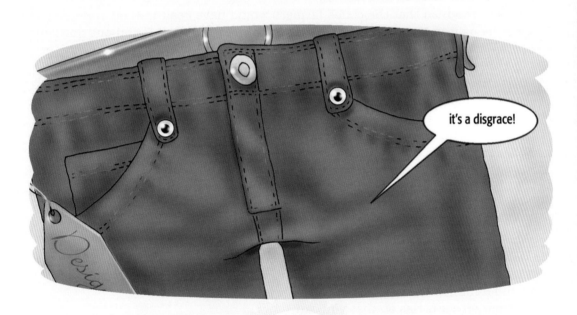

it's a disgrace!

EXAMINER'S TOP TIPS

• This scenario could describe any manufactured product in the shops today. It is rare for a product to be manufactured in only one location from components that are sourced locally.

• A solution to the exploitation of workers in LEDCs is to stop buying the goods. But this would have the effect of making those people unemployed.

• A more effective solution is to campaign for workers to be given a fair wage and acceptable working conditions. Most Transnational Companies (TNCs) are very concerned about their public image as this affects sales and ultimately their profits.

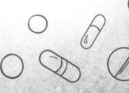

Full of beans?

Coffee Drinkers' Club
Weston-super-Mare
Avon
UK

From the Social Secretary

Dear Members,

It is with great sadness and considerable regret that I am writing to inform you that I am resigning from my position as Social Secretary, with immediate effect.

I'm sure you are aware that we have just returned from our annual Coffee Drinkers' Club holiday to Kafe in Ethiopia, the birthplace of coffee. We left in anticipation of visiting the farmers and fields where coffee was discovered. We have come back shocked and horrified, with a bitter taste in our mouths.

We had imagined that the coffee farmers would have been well off and delighted to welcome us into their comfortable modern homes. We soon found out that only a fraction of the price paid for coffee in this country goes to the poor farmers in LEDCs. In some instances that is less than 2% of the price of a jar.

The effect that this has on Ethiopia is hard to describe. Seven hundred households, approximately 15 million people, depend on coffee for everything. We

met families living in one-roomed mud huts with nothing to live on. They had taken their children out of school because they couldn't afford to pay the fees. They had sold their animals to pay for essentials and they had cut back on their food intake to save money.

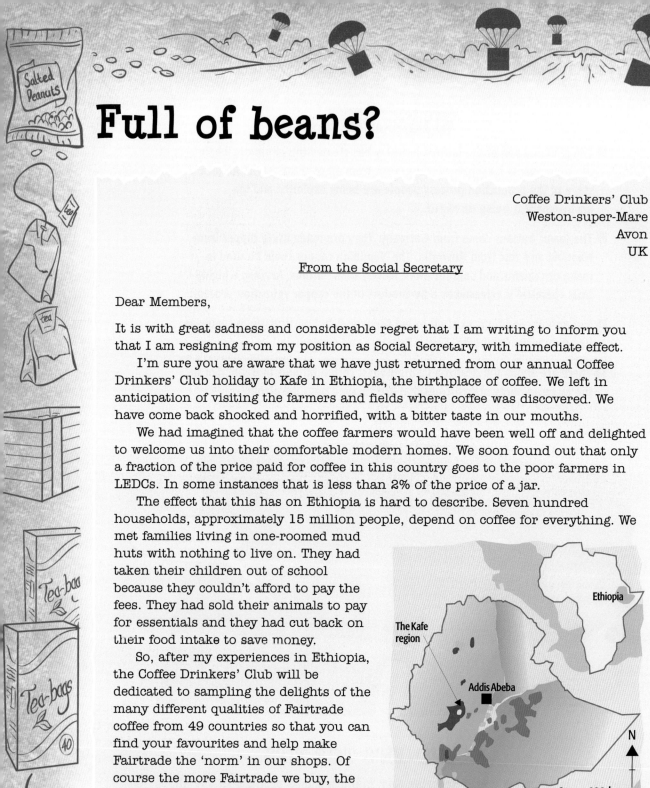

So, after my experiences in Ethiopia, the Coffee Drinkers' Club will be dedicated to sampling the delights of the many different qualities of Fairtrade coffee from 49 countries so that you can find your favourites and help make Fairtrade the 'norm' in our shops. Of course the more Fairtrade we buy, the more the coffee farmers and their families have the opportunity to improve their lives.

Yours in humility,

Veronica Hawthorne

Veronica Hawthorne (Mrs)

FAIRTRADE

Guarantees
a **better deal**
for Third World
Producers

Look for this Mark on Fairtrade products
www.fairtrade.org.uk

KEY FACTS

- Coffee sales worldwide equal £24.3 billion.

- Nestlé and Starbucks have seen their profits rise by as much as 41% recently.

- The price of coffee received by farmers has fallen by 50% in three years.

- Most families in Kafe live on less than £56.50 a year.

- Two children out every ten are destined to die from a preventable disease before they are five years old.

- The Fairtrade company, Cafédirect, buys its coffee from smallholder farmer co-operatives and other producer organisations across 11 countries for 90p per pound. This guarantees a fair price, stable income and a better life for the coffee growers involved.

EXAMINER'S TOP TIP

Farming and food production is more globalised than you might think. TNCs like Nestlé and Brooke Bond are responsible for the majority of the food in our shops; small local producers are becoming increasingly rare.

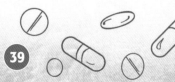
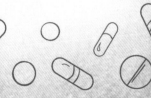

800 million people are hungry. 300 million of them are children.

24,000 people die of starvation daily.

HEALTH

Overeating in MEDCs causes obesity and heart disease.

54,000 people in the UK have HIV.

28 million people in Africa have HIV.

Life expectancy in Malawi is 38. In the UK it is 79.

DEVELO

75 million people worldwide depend on coffee farming.

85% of people of working age in Malawi are farmers.

Less than 2% of the price of instant coffee goes to the coffee farmers.

FARMING

76% of Malawi's exports are tobacco.

Peanut farmers in Senegal are not earning enough to meet their basic needs.

Fairtrade ensures that farmers receive a fair price for their produce and good working conditions.

Cotton farmers in Benin earn 60p a day.

FAIRTRADE

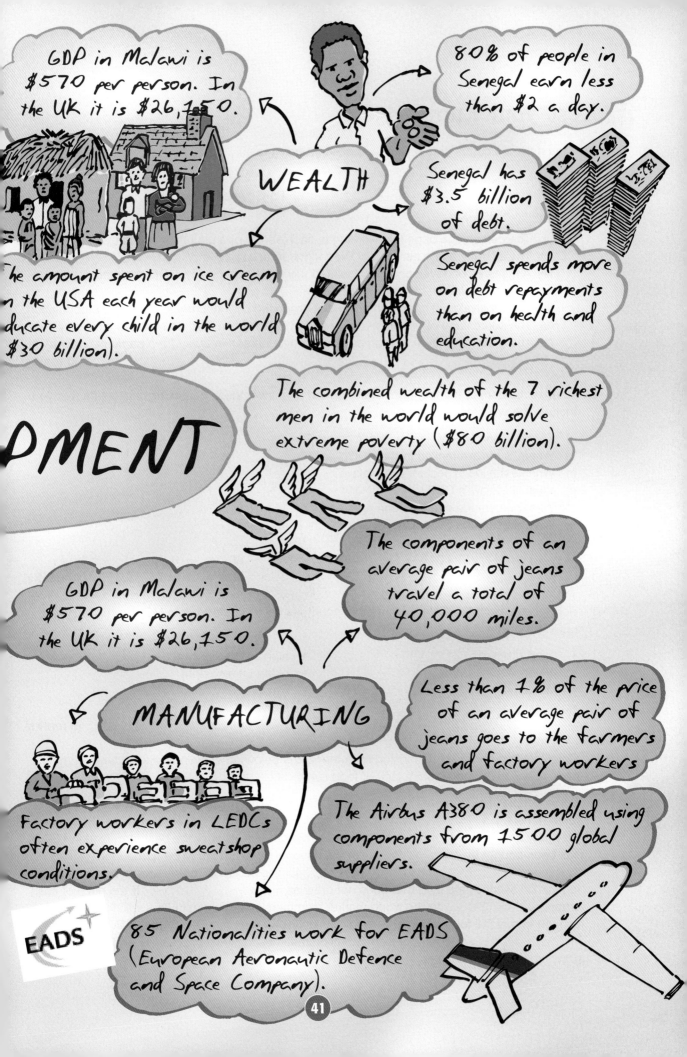

GDP in Malawi is $570 per person. In the UK it is $26,150.

80% of people in Senegal earn less than $2 a day.

WEALTH

Senegal has $3.5 billion of debt.

The amount spent on ice cream in the USA each year would educate every child in the world ($30 billion).

Senegal spends more on debt repayments than on health and education.

The combined wealth of the 7 richest men in the world would solve extreme poverty ($80 billion).

PMENT

The components of an average pair of jeans travel a total of 40,000 miles.

GDP in Malawi is $570 per person. In the UK it is $26,750.

MANUFACTURING

Less than 7% of the price of an average pair of jeans goes to the farmers and factory workers

Factory workers in LEDCs often experience sweatshop conditions.

The Airbus A380 is assembled using components from 1500 global suppliers.

EADS

85 Nationalities work for EADS (European Aeronautic Defence and Space Company).

Test your knowledge 2

1 Match the indicators (a to f) with their descriptions (i to vi).

a) HDI
b) GDP
c) Life expectancy
d) Adult literacy
e) Employment structure
f) Calorific intake

(i)   The percentage of people working in each sector of a country's economy.
(ii) The average age a person will live to in a particular country.
(iii) A measure of development calculated using life expectancy, GDP, adult literacy and school enrolment; created by the UN
(iv) The total value of goods and services produced by a country, divided by its population.
(v)   The percentage of people over the age of 18 who can read and write in a country.
(vi) The average amount of food consumed by a person in a day for a particular country.

(6 marks)

2 Choose the correct number from the selection to answer these questions (make sure that you include the units for each number).

a) For how long was Malawi a British colony?
b) Where is Malawi ranked in the HDI?
c) What is the life expectancy in Malawi?
d) What is Malawi's GDP?
e) What percentage of adults can read and write in Malawi?
f) What percentage of people in Malawi work in agriculture?

60   165   75   38   85   570

(6 marks)

3 Sort these descriptions of problems that countries have with food, into MEDC problems and LEDC problems.

- heart disease
- malnourishment
- hunger
- obesity
- high blood pressure
- being underweight
- waste
- starvation

(8 marks)

4 Complete this paragraph (choosing from the words below) to explain why such large numbers of people in LEDCs die from a lack of food every day.

Some people in LEDCs are .... farmers. This means that they grow their own food. If there is a .... or their crops are attacked by disease or ...., they may not be able to grow enough to meet their needs. A lot of the best farm land in LEDCs has been bought by .... or the national government, to be farmed for .... This creates .... for the economy, but results in people having to farm on second-rate land that does not grow as much .... If the price of cash crops .... on the world market, commercial farmers in LEDCs will not make enough to buy the food required to feed themselves or their families. Some LEDCs are involved in .... or other conflicts, which sometimes makes it impossible for farmers to grow crops or raise animals.

cash crops pests subsistence food

drought falls money TNCs (Transnational Corporations) civil wars

(9 marks)

5 Use the world map to match up the country with the component of a pair of jeans (below).

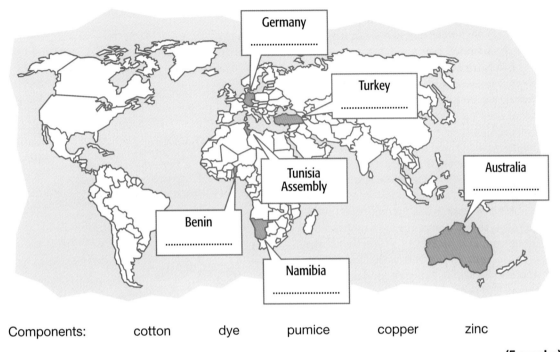

Germany
....

Turkey
....

Tunisia
Assembly

Australia
....

Benin
....

Namibia
....

Components: cotton dye pumice copper zinc

(5 marks)

6 Describe the working conditions for the people involved in the manufacture of a pair of jeans. (Aim to write at least one description for each country illustrated in question 5).

(5 marks)

7 Why do you think the components and manufacturing of a pair of jeans is so spread out around the world?

(3 marks)

8 Read the double pages about farming coffee and peanuts. Write a list of the similarities and differences between these two examples of LEDC agriculture. (Try to find at least three similarities and three differences.)

(6 marks)

9 How can global trade and/or manufacturing be made fairer for all those involved?

(4 marks)

10 Why are there such wide differences in quality of life between LEDCs and MEDCs? Hint: divide your answer into physical and human reasons.

(8 marks)

(Total 60 marks)

Tour de France

Dear Mum and Dad

I am nearly at the end of my three weeks with Etienne. I have had the most amazing French exchange ever.

Etienne's Dad picked me up from the airport in Geneva. It was weird to start a French exchange by flying to Switzerland. We drove over the border to their chalet in the French Alps near Annecy. Most of the Dugas family gather there every year. It was a shock having the evening meal together on a long table in the garden. Everyone spoke at once, and just about all I managed was 'bonjour'!

After a week in the French Alps I said goodbye to Mt Blanc, France's highest mountain, and we drove to Biarritz to stay with the rest of the family. Our journey took us across the Rhône, France's longest river, at Lyons, the second largest city in France. From there we drove west over the Massif Central, a mountainous region of France formed from extinct volcanoes. The final leg of the trip took us through the foothills of the Pyrennes, before reaching our destination.

We travelled about 700 kms. The heat was quite amazing – the closer we got to the south west coast of France the hotter it became. The thermometer in the car read 15°C in the Alps and it rose to 30°C at Biarritz. We drank gallons of bottled water to keep us cool.

Tomorrow we are leaving Biarritz to head back to the Dugas' own home in Evry – a new town on the outskirts of Paris. They have promised me at least a day to wander around the city. I'm desperate to go up the Eiffel Tower and I would love to go on a boat trip along the Seine.

I'm not looking forward to another long journey in the car. We'll cross the Garonne and Loire rivers on the way, and the family have told me we'll go through some of the most beautiful valleys in France such as the Dordogne. They've also warned me that the landscape of the Paris Basin is not as spectacular; mainly low lying, which is great for farming and industry, but not so good for tourists.

À bientôt!

Andrew

KEY FACTS

⬅ France is 547 030 km² – more than twice the area of the UK.

➡ The Rhône is one of Europe's longest rivers at 800 km long.

⬇ France contains Europe's highest mountain, Mt Blanc, which is 4807 m high.

⬆ France's relief varies considerably throughout the country. The north of France is relatively flat, particularly around Paris. However, there are many major river valleys, such as those of the Rhône, Loire, Garonne and Dordogne. France has three main highland regions, the Alps, the Massif Central and the Pyrenees, and smaller highland regions such as the Jura mountains and the Vosges to the east.

⬅ The highland areas have a climate that is typical of upland locations; temperatures are lower than average and rainfall is higher.

➡ The regions of Languedoc and Provence on the south coast of France have a Mediterranean climate. Summer and winter temperatures are the highest in France, and the area is characterised by vegetation that has adapted to the long dry summers that this area experiences.

⬇ The north east coast of France has a climate that is relatively similar to Britain's, as it is affected by the Atlantic ocean bringing plenty of rain.

⬆ The central regions have a more continental climate, which is characterised by cold winters and hot summers.

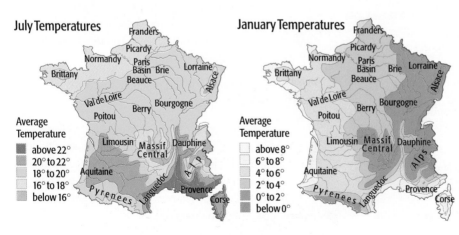

EXAMINER'S TOP TIP

A good way to learn the physical features of a country is to practise drawing them on a blank map. Use these pages to learn France's geography, close the book, then add the rivers, high land and low land on an outline map you have already prepared.

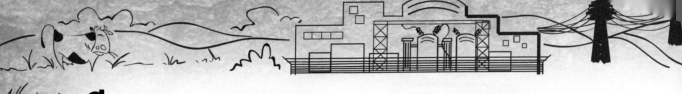

Sour grapes

Jean and Louis sat at a table outside the café and surveyed the scene before them. Never in their short time in the Narbonne <u>Gendarmerie</u> had they experienced such violence. The street before them was littered with concrete blocks, burnt out boxes, litter bins and anything else the protesters could set fire to. The Languedoc-Roussillon region had never experienced anything like it.

They could have understood it if it had of been a demonstration against the war in Iraq or the proposed changes to the <u>European Union</u> (<u>EU</u>) constitution. Instead, the destruction had been caused by rioting wine makers.

Philippe Vergnes, the president of the wine makers' union, had explained why the 7000 wine makers were protesting in a speech at the start of the day. The price of French wine had fallen by 30% that year and sales had fallen by the same proportion. 267 million bottles of wine were destined to be turned into industrial alcohol, because no one was buying them.

The wine regions of France

Foreign competition was a major factor in the decline of the local wine industry. In the UK, sales of Australian wine had recently over taken those of France. France exports 1.78 billion bottles of wine a year, fewer than the 1.93 billion bottles from the '<u>New World</u>' producers of California, Chile and Australia combined.

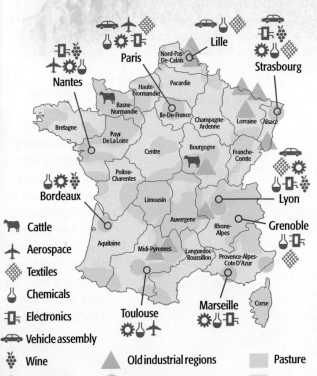

Cattle
Aerospace
Textiles
Chemicals
Electronics
Vehicle assembly
Wine
Engineering

Old industrial regions
Main metropolitan areas

Pasture
Crop

Jean and Louis watched as the first street cleaners of the afternoon arrived to begin the clear up. Perhaps the government should be supporting the wine makers in these hard times. However, the situation was nothing new. Primary sector and secondary sector jobs had been declining in France for some years. In 1954 30% of the working population worked in farming, the same proportion worked in manufacturing. Currently just 4% of the workers were in farming and 26% in manufacturing. The tertiary sector was struggling to keep up.

Unemployment had reached 10% across the country.

<u>Services</u> were the jobs of the future: police, education, retail, leisure and tourism, etc. As Jean and Louis left the café, to make their way home to a shower and change of clothes, they knew that their jobs were safe. As safe as they could be... until the next riot.

◄ France's economy has changed in the last 50 years in much the same way as the UK's, along with the rest of the countries in Western Europe and North America:

◄ Employment in the primary sector has continued to decline.

◄ Employment in the secondary sector has declined dramatically (deindustrialisation).

◄ Employment in the tertiary and quaternary sector has risen (tertiarisation and reindustrialisation), with five million new jobs created in this sector since 1970.

◄ The changes in the country's employment structure have affected each region of France to different degrees:

- Aricultural regions such as Brittany, the Auvergne, and Centre have suffered falling incomes and de-population.

- Traditional manufacturing regions such as Nord Pas de Calais, Lorraine and Midi-Pyrenees have also experienced recession, due to the concentrations of population the impacts of unemployment and decline have been more extreme.

- Regions characterised by the service industry or high tech industry have made some progress in terms of employment and wealth. These include the Île de France (the Paris region), Languedoc-Roussillon and Provence-Alpes-Côte d'Azur.

	1960	1980	2001
Primary	22%	9.4%	5.2% (1 m people)
Secondary	29.1%	24.8%	17.7% (4 m people)
Tertiary	48.9%	65.8%	77.1% (18 m people)

NB: France's working population was 26 million in 2001, 45% of the total population. Of the 26 million, approximately 2.5 million were unemployed (roughly 10%).

EXAMINER'S TOP TIPS

To explain the changes in employment you need to include a number of reasons:

• Globalisation: LEDCs and Newly Industrialising Countries (NICs) are able to produce agricultural and manufactured goods more cheaply and efficiently than France.

• Technology: Machinery, particularly computers and robots, have made farming and manufacturing more efficient and less dependent on human employees.

• Social changes: People in France are more skilled and educated, so they want to work in the tertiary and quaternary sectors. Demand for leisure, tourism and entertainment has grown, which leads to a greater demand for employees in these sectors.

Pastures new

Le Compte de Beauchamps looked out over the Champs Elysées from his library window. His grey hair was lit by the low evening sun, dust swirled in the air. Gradually, as the sun dipped below the Arc de Triomphe, he turned to me and spoke.

'I will not miss Paris. It's no longer my home – I just don't recognise it. The city where I grew up, and where my father and his father grew up, is not the city out there.'

I shifted my weight from one foot to the other. The developers would be arriving within the hour. I had to get the old man into a taxi and to Charles de Gaulle airport before then.

'It's just not the place I knew,' he continued. 'We still have the Eiffel Tower, the Louvre and Nôtre Dame Cathedral. The Seine still flows. But where are all the French?'

He picked up a copy of *Le Monde* from the table and threw it at me.

'Look!' He blustered, 'Twenty per cent of the population is from overseas – that's 180 000 people. There are fewer and fewer French people living here every day!'

'Well, they're welcome to it! And don't get me started on that 'La Défense' place.' He rocked to his feet. 'La Grande Arche! I call it La Grande Ar...' He was interrupted by my mobile ringing.

The taxi had arrived just in the nick of time. He and I both knew that the sale of his Paris apartment would more than cover the cost of converting the family château in the Loire Valley. After 900 years of protecting the French aristocracy from invaders, it was to become an upmarket bed and breakfast destination for the more discerning traveller.

'Come on then,' he grumbled as he walked towards the door, 'let's head off.'

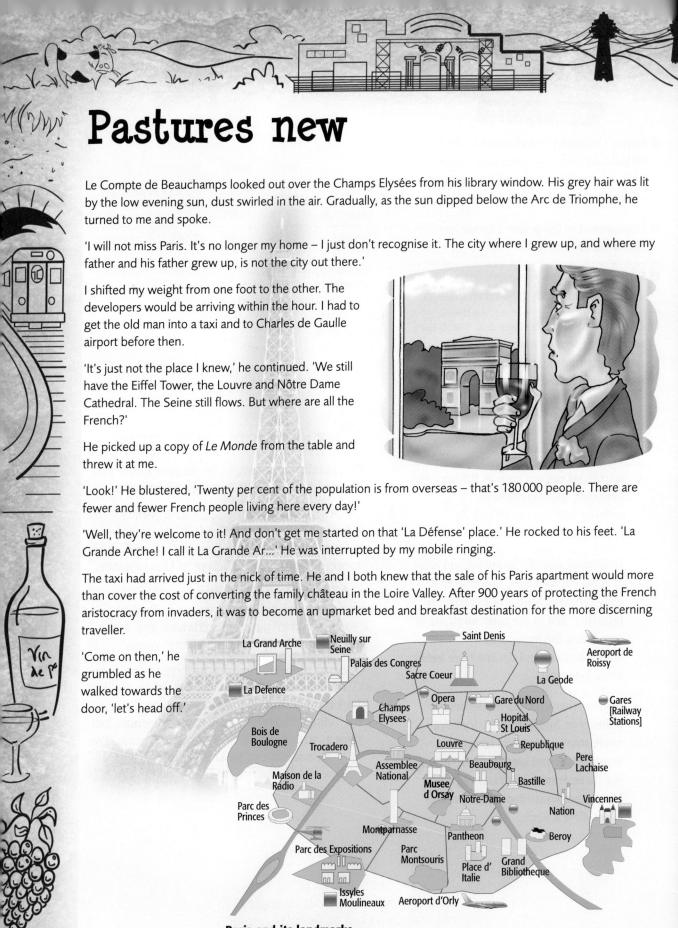

Paris and its landmarks

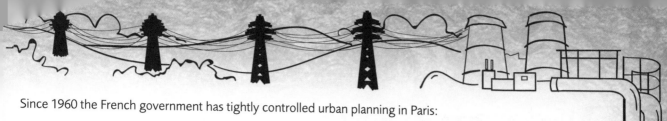

Since 1960 the French government has tightly controlled urban planning in Paris:

- Five new towns have been built.
- New roads have been constructed, including the Boulevard Péripherique, an inner ring road.
- The Métro has been extended to reach the suburbs.
- A regional express train, the <u>RER</u>, has been created.
- New industrial estates have been developed at the edge of the city.
- Charles de Gaulle airport has been built.

The Stade de France was constructed on the outskirts of Paris for the Football World Cup in 1998, with a capacity of 80 000 people.

La Défense is a business, housing, cultural and retail development 8 km north of the central business district (CBD). It provides 80 000 jobs and is expected to have a final population of 60 000. The Grande Arche de la Défense is a 100 m x 100 m office block in the shape of a cube with the middle part left open. It attracts 1.2 million tourists a year.

Marne la Vallée is a new town of approximately 100 000 people, built 13 km east of Paris. It is described as a 'garden town' that manages to mix businesses with a pleasant environment. Disneyland Paris is located here and in 2003 12 million visitors passed through its gates.

KEY FACTS

◁ **Paris covers an area of 104 km².**

▷ **Paris dominates France. It contains 20% of French jobs and produces 30% of France's exports.**

▽ **Its population is 2.1 million. This is less than its peak population in 1920 of 2.9 million. Since 1963 500 000 people have left Paris.**

△ **Paris does have problems: pollution, inefficient public transport, huge traffic jams at rush hour and high costs of living in the city.**

◁ **Paris is one of the world's most visited cities, with approximately seven million tourist visits a year.**

La Grand Arche

EXAMINER'S TOP TIP

Urban areas are often described as being 'dynamic', which means that they are constantly changing. In an exam or test you may be asked to describe, explain or assess the impact of urban change.

Nuts and bolts

It was the end of Luc's first day of work experience. His friends had all laughed at him when he had told them that he had found his dream job at Beck-Crespel; a specialist fixtures manufacturer just 20 miles from their home town of Lille. 'Nuts and bolts factory!' they had jeered. But he knew that in Nord Pas de Calais, where unemployment was 12%, you couldn't afford to be choosy.

He had coped with the usual jokes played on new work experience students. He had been to the warehouse to look for a box of 10 mm holes, and burst in on an important meeting after being told the room was the staff toilet. All in all, he felt that he hadn't done too badly.

Luc's great-grandfather had been a coal miner before the Second World War; that was when the region was at its peak. Luc's grandfather had worked in the steel industry.

The economic decline had begun during the 1950s. Between 1970 and 1980 12 000 steel workers lost their jobs.

Luc's father had a job; he was an engineer at the Eurostar terminal in the city. Luc was proud that his father was contributing to the <u>regeneration</u> of Lille. Despite the high unemployment, the £30 million <u>regional aid</u> that the French government had poured into the region was having an effect.

Lille was beginning to live up to its planned image as a Eurometropolis and crossroads of Europe. Judging by the numbers of tourists and new roads, houses, shops and entertainment, Lille was getting back on its feet. The factory was ideally located – Lille's central position in Europe made it easy for the factory to supply other manufacturing industries.

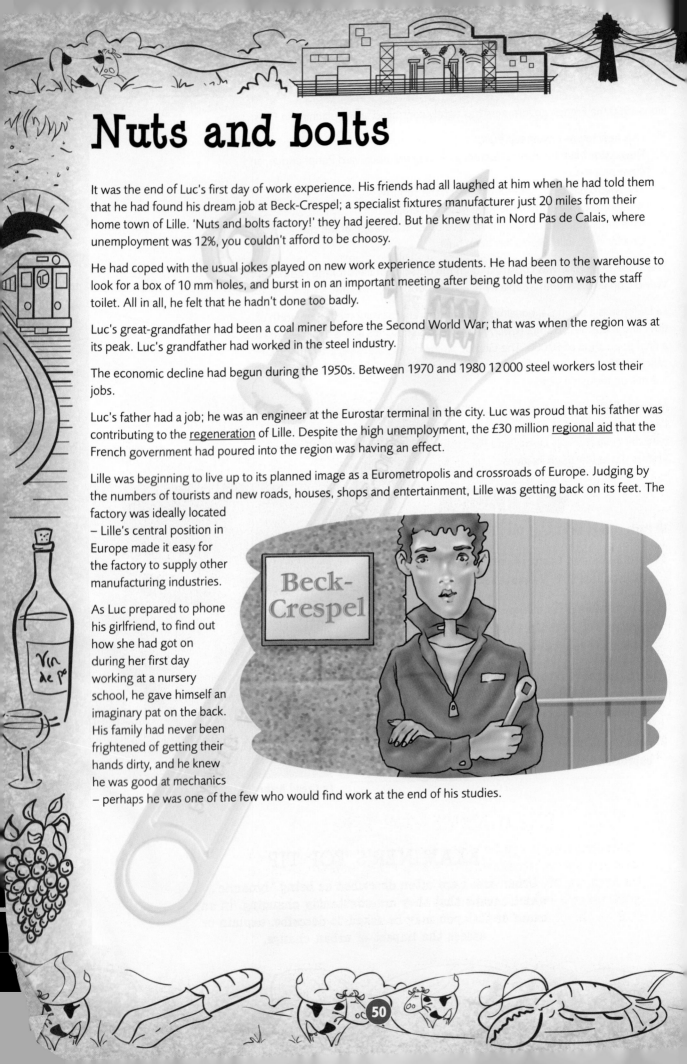

As Luc prepared to phone his girlfriend, to find out how she had got on during her first day working at a nursery school, he gave himself an imaginary pat on the back. His family had never been frightened of getting their hands dirty, and he knew he was good at mechanics – perhaps he was one of the few who would find work at the end of his studies.

◄ The Nord Pas de Calais region used to be the industrial heartland of France. Lille became the fourth largest city in France.

➡ The abundance of coal and iron ore had caused rapid industrialisation in much the same way as it had happened in South Wales and the North of England.

⬇ The government's regeneration plan involved improving the environment, particularly in Lille, and providing jobs through the attraction of new industry.

⬆ Central to the success of the plan was the Eurostar terminal. Lille is marketed as the tourist and business crossroads of Europe.

◄ Beck-Crespel employs 359 workers at Armentiers, 20 miles from Lille. It exports parts for power stations and the oil industry, mainly to China and India.

Lille's Eurostar terminal

EXAMINER'S TOP TIPS

Industrial change can be explained by using a combination of internal and external factors. Internal factors originate from the country involved, such as labour costs and the role of the government; external factors come from outside the country, such as the effect of TNCs and newly industrialised countries.

Selfish shellfish?

Jean-Pierre is France's longest-lived and most intelligent oyster. He is a filter-feeder. Jean-Pierre has spent most of his life on the bottom of a pool, sucking in and digesting anything edible that passes by. Fortunately for Jean-Pierre, his particular pool is in Mt St Michel Bay, just off the coast from Cancale, one of the leading oyster producing towns in Brittany.

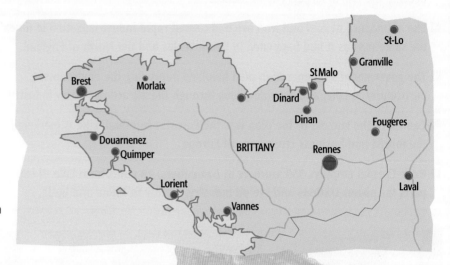

Jean-Pierre is a self-taught expert in <u>conchyliculture</u>. The oyster pools in Mt St Michel Bay benefit from one of the largest tides in the world – every day the sea rises and retreats on average 15–20 km. The tide carries with it sediments from rivers and the sea bed, ideal food for oysters. The tidal range also makes it easy for the oyster and mussel farmers to drive their tractors onto the sea bed to harvest the shellfish.

Brittany, as well as producing mussels and oysters, is one of France's most important <u>agricultural</u> areas. It produces two thirds of France's animal products and contains, half of the country's pigs and a quarter of the poultry and cattle.

The huge numbers of livestock produce equally large amounts of <u>manure</u>. This has traditionally been used as a fertiliser on fields. The manure has been washed into rivers and some people are saying that drinking water sources have been <u>polluted</u> and coastal <u>estuaries</u> are being killed by the extra algae that the manure is causing to grow.

This isn't a problem for Jean-Pierre, since oysters are not fussy. The nutrient-rich <u>runoff</u> from the fields, which is delivered to Mt St Michel Bay via Brittany's rivers, is an ideal source of food.

The French government is building water filtration plants in Brittany and encouraging farmers to farm fewer animals. This should solve the pollution problems, but Jean-Pierre is worried his future could become uncertain. However, he is realistic; he knows that it is only a matter of time before it is his turn to grace the table at one of the region's top restaurants.

◄ Brittany has a unique history. It was once separate from France and has its own language and culture.

➡ Brittany has 9000 hectares of breeding pools producing over 30 000 tonnes of oysters a year – a quarter of France's total oyster production.

⬇ 10 million tourists visit Brittany each year. It has 1000 km of <u>coast</u>, and its mild climate and sandy beaches draw people from all over Europe.

⬆ As with other farming regions, Brittany has suffered from employment problems. However, tourism, changes in farming practices and government support is bringing prosperity back to the region.

Brittany has its own language and culture

EXAMINER'S TOP TIPS

Shellfish farming, like all farming, is affected by human and physical factors. Physical factors relate to the natural environment, for example temperature, precipitation, wind, relief, soil quality and (in the case of oyster farming) tides. Human factors are those determined by people, including labour, transport, markets/consumers, government policies and international prices.

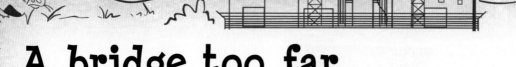

A bridge too far

Madame du Bois sat in her rocking chair, knitting. Beside her, balanced awkwardly on an old milking stool, sat Claudette d'Avignon. Her laptop balanced precariously on her lap. Claudette wondered what to do. If there was a national award for stubbornness, Madame du Bois would have won it for the last two years in a row. Claudette was her company's best negotiator; she could not fail where many had.

The road had to be built. How else could the half dozen villages be connected to the new A75 Montpellier to Clermont Ferrand autoroute? The only thing preventing the construction company moving in was a small farm, owned by a certain Antoinette du Bois.

Before the A75, the Auvergne region had been an economic backwater. The region was mountainous, with few major roads and few jobs outside the farming sector. The A75 had breathed new life into this part of France. Thanks to the road, new businesses had set up in the region and tourism has flourished.

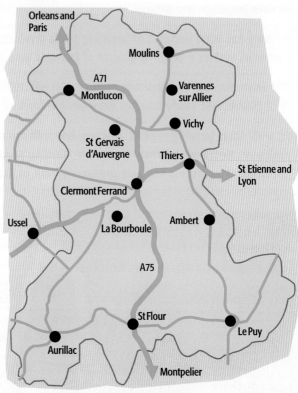

The A75 and the Auvergne region

Claudette's argument was that it was pure selfishness to deny this part of the Auvergne the chance to develop in line with the rest of the region. Madame du Bois had argued that she liked things to stay as they were. She had pointed out the 28 metre high artificial volcano at Vulcania, Europe's latest volcano theme park, which now dominated the view from her balcony. Madame du Bois had claimed that she did not want to be responsible for enabling something like that to be built where her sheep had used to graze.

Secretly Claudette agreed with her, but as she left, promising to return in a few days, she felt that she was fighting a losing battle.

Madame du Bois watched the back of the BMW bounce its way down the track leading from her farm. She chuckled to herself as she picked up the latest copy of the local property paper. Just a few more days... then I'll sell, she thought to herself.

KEY FACTS

◄ The Auvergne is located in the Massif Central, the area of highland found to the south in France.

➔ It covers an area of 26 013 km².

⬇ It has a population of 1 308 878 people – just 2.2% of the total population of France.

⬆ The Auvergne is famous for its extinct volcanoes. They can be seen on any bottle of Volvic mineral water, which is produced in the region.

◄ 60% of the Auvergne is farmland, 10% of the working population are farmers.

➔ Construction on the new road began in1988. Now that the 360 km are complete, the region has been opened up.

⬇ Craft industries and tourism have begun to flourish. The Auvergne now boasts 1250 hotels, 350 campsites and 2400 gîtes (holiday homes).

The Auvergne's extinct volcanoes

The Millan Viaduct carrying the A75 through the Massif Central

EXAMINER'S TOP TIP

• Since the 1960s the French government has followed a policy of decentralisation. This is deliberately encouraging people and businesses away from Paris and the relatively wealthy north of France, towards the less well off southern regions.

• Decentralisation has involved relocating some government establishments elsewhere. For example, French bank notes are now printed in Clermont Ferrand. It has also involved improving transport across France, such as building new roads and railway lines.

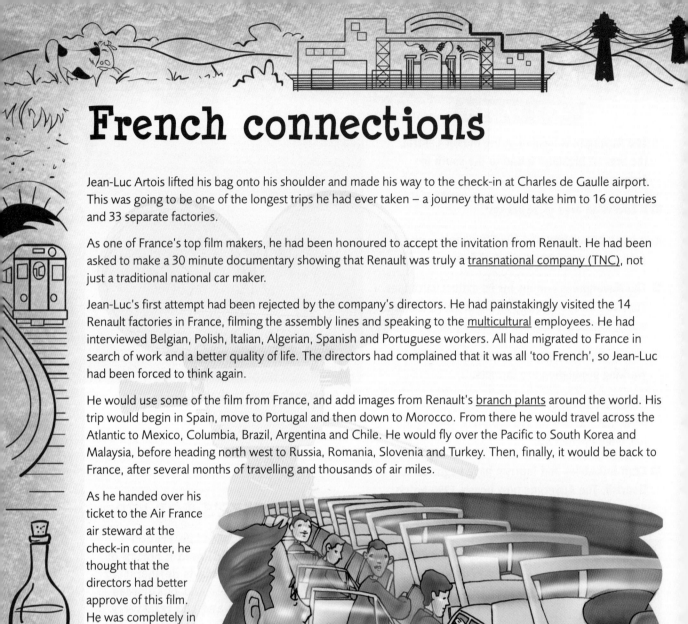

French connections

Jean-Luc Artois lifted his bag onto his shoulder and made his way to the check-in at Charles de Gaulle airport. This was going to be one of the longest trips he had ever taken – a journey that would take him to 16 countries and 33 separate factories.

As one of France's top film makers, he had been honoured to accept the invitation from Renault. He had been asked to make a 30 minute documentary showing that Renault was truly a <u>transnational company (TNC)</u>, not just a traditional national car maker.

Jean-Luc's first attempt had been rejected by the company's directors. He had painstakingly visited the 14 Renault factories in France, filming the assembly lines and speaking to the <u>multicultural</u> employees. He had interviewed Belgian, Polish, Italian, Algerian, Spanish and Portuguese workers. All had migrated to France in search of work and a better quality of life. The directors had complained that it was all 'too French', so Jean-Luc had been forced to think again.

He would use some of the film from France, and add images from Renault's <u>branch plants</u> around the world. His trip would begin in Spain, move to Portugal and then down to Morocco. From there he would travel across the Atlantic to Mexico, Columbia, Brazil, Argentina and Chile. He would fly over the Pacific to South Korea and Malaysia, before heading north west to Russia, Romania, Slovenia and Turkey. Then, finally, it would be back to France, after several months of travelling and thousands of air miles.

As he handed over his ticket to the Air France air steward at the check-in counter, he thought that the directors had better approve of this film. He was completely in favour of <u>globalisation</u> and the spread of French economic activity world wide. He just didn't fancy the thought of hours spent cooped up in the cabin of various aircraft, eating food from plastic trays for nothing.

Renault branch plants around the world

KEY FACTS

◁ France could be described as one of the most globalised countries in the world.

◁ It owns 120 000 km² of territory world wide, containing 2.2 million people.

◁ There are four territories that are counted as full French *départements* (administrative regions), in spite of being miles away from France. These are:
- – Guadeloupe
- – Martinique
- – Réunion
- – French Guiana.

⬆ France also owns 150 islands of French Polynesia and it claims a significant portion of Antarctica.

◁ France has a long history of welcoming immigrants; this currently stands at a rate of 62 000 arrivals a year.

➡ In 2000, 7.4% of the French population (4.3 million people) was classed as from overseas.

⬇ Most migrants work in construction, the car industry or the service sector.

⬆ Foreign trade accounts for 28% of France's GNP. France is fortunate that it has a <u>trade surplus</u> that is growing.

◁ France has 15 788 <u>subsidiaries</u> operating overseas, employing 2 545 000 people.

➡ 2860 foreign TNCs can be found in France, accounting for 28% of France's economic output and 24% of jobs.

EXAMINER'S TOP TIPS

Welcoming immigrants brings many benefits to the host countries.

- Most immigrants fill vacancies in key sectors of the economy.

- They bring a rich variety of music, food, fashion and other cultural attributes.

- They create connections and understanding between the countries of the world.

An in tents meeting

The circus had arrived on the outskirts of Avignon, near to the Pont du Gard. It was a location the circus had used for generations during its summer tour through Provence. Madame L'étrange set up her tent and waited patiently.

The young man was her first customer. His question was simple and direct: 'What does the future hold for France?'

Madame L'étrange gazed into the crystal ball and began to speak. 'I see space rockets, helicopters and aeroplanes. I see tall chimneys, concrete spheres, containers; but no smoke. I see all colours and sizes of vehicles. I see trains.'

The young man's face lit up. 'Yes, the rocket must be the Ariane 5 ECA, the helicopter will be the Eurocopter AS350 B3, the plane will be the Airbus A380, and I guess the train will be the latest generation of the TGV.'

He hardly paused for breath.

'The chimneys will be from our nuclear power stations. The cars will be Renaults, Peugeots and Citroens.'

Madame L'étrange was encouraged, and more images began to emerge.

'I see happy and prosperous French people. I see clean air and water. I see mountains, forests and rivers full of wildlife, being enjoyed by all.'

The young man agreed, 'France has the fourth largest economy in the world and is 16th in the HDI. We spend 1% of the nation's wealth on protecting the environment. Well over six million hectares are protected as National Parks, Regional Parks or nature reserves. The government is committed to sustainable growth.'

This was all very well, but Madame L'étrange could tell that so far she had failed to answer the young man's question. 'Tell me,' she said, 'what is it exactly that you wish to know?'

His anxious expression returned, 'France is the name of a horse in the 2.30 pm race. I've bet €10 000 on it and I was actually hoping you'd be able to tell me whether it will win before my wife finds out.'

◄ France is a world leader in aerospace engineering. The European space launch pad is located in French Guyana in South America.

☐➡ France generates 77% of its electricity from nuclear power, and is a world leader in nuclear power generation and reprocessing.

☐⬇ France is one of the lowest contributors to global warming out of all the industrialised nations. It produces 6.3 tonnes per capita of CO_2, compared with the UK's 9.2 tonnes and the US's 19.8 tonnes.

☐⬆ France is the second largest exporter of services, food and agricultural products in the world.

◄ France accounts for 5% of the world's economic output and 6% of world trade.

➡ France employs 400 000 people in environmental protection.

⬊ 85% of the country's 5500 km of coastline meets international standards of cleanliness.

An Ariane rocket

The TGV

A Eurocopter

An Airbus

EXAMINER'S TOP TIP

Sustainable development is a key concept in geography. It describes a condition where meeting the needs of the current generation of people does not affect the ability of future generations to meet their own needs. It seeks to ensure a better quality of life for everyone, now and for generations to come, and it encompasses environmental, social and economic goals.

The population of France is 59.5 million.

10% of the working population of France is unemployed.

6% of French people live in towns and cities.

PEOPLE

7.4% of the population of France is from another country.

Paris is the capital of France. Its population is 2.7 million.

VCE

Paris is one of Europe's most visited cities.

The Auvergne has 7250 hotels and 350 campsites

Renault owns 33 factories in 76 countries.

788 foreign companies employ 24% of French workers.

TOURISM

70 million tourists visit Brittany every year.

MANUFACTURING

Lille is marketing itself as a tourist 'crossroads' of Europe.

FERME

igh tech manufacturing growing in rance.

Traditional manufacturing is declining France.

Secondary industry employs 47.7% of France's working population

Tertiary industry employs 77.7% of France's working population.

Test your knowledge 3

1 Complete the word search by finding the answers to the following questions:

a) The highest mountain in France.
b) The longest river in France.
c) The river that flows through Paris.
d) The mountain range that borders France and Spain.
e) The mountain range that borders France and Switzerland.
f) The area of lowland found to the north of France.
g) The sea on the west coast of France.
h) The sea on the south coast of France.

R	T	N	I	S	A	B	S	I	R	A	P	S	Z
A	H	P	L	O	Y	H	N	B	M	R	L	L	P
M	S	O	R	B	C	P	A	T	V	K	P	P	B
P	E	O	N	N	E	W	B	H	P	L	B	V	S
O	I	V	G	E	M	L	U	M	R	F	C	B	N
J	N	A	E	N	A	R	R	E	T	I	D	E	M
W	E	N	P	N	M	K	G	H	J	R	C	V	M
Y	I	N	C	P	C	I	T	N	A	L	T	A	C
R	P	Y	R	E	N	E	E	S	W	Q	Z	U	O

(8 marks)

2 Match the employment sectors with the correct figures and descriptions.

Primary	77.1	Manufacturing raw materials into products.
Secondary	5.2	Providing a service to people.
Tertiary	17.7	The extraction of resources from the land or sea.

(6 marks)

3 Using the paragraph below, explain why the percentage of people in France employed in the secondary sector has fallen.

Traditional manufacturing in France, such as the manufacture of ...., has lost jobs for three main reasons. People are buying manufactured goods from other countries, particularly from .... in SE Asia, rather than France. This is because those countries are able to produce similar products, which are .... and .... than French products. Advances in technology have resulted in .... taking the place of .... People are more skilled and educated in France, they prefer to work in the .... or in research and development than in .... They may also be able to earn .... wages in these sectors.

machines   labour   service sector   better   iron and steel

cheaper   manufacturing   newly industrialised countries   higher

(9 marks)

4 Divide this list into the advantages and disadvantages of living in Paris.

Congestion
Culture and entertainment
A lot going on
Overcrowded

Employment
Pollution
Expensive living costs
Connections to the rest of France/Europe/the World

(8 marks)

5   How have the French authorities acted to improve the quality of life in Paris? (Try to include information about housing, employment, transport, services and the environment in your answer.)

(5 marks)

6   Which three of these statements describe Brittany?

•   A region of extinct volcanoes.
•   Produces two thirds of France's animal products.
•   Has 1000 km of coastline.
•   Used to be an economic backwater.
•   Has ten million tourists a year

(Which region fits with the remaining two statements?)

(4 marks)

7   Explain why Brittany used to suffer from severe water pollution. How has the problem of water pollution been reduced in the last few years?

(4 marks)

8   Name the places on the world map with connections to France.

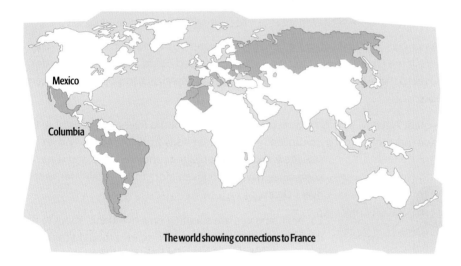

The world showing connections to France

(9 marks)

9   Give arguments for and against immigration into France.

(6 marks)

10 How might the future success of France be dependent on its connections with the rest of the world?

(6 marks)

(Total 65 marks)

Getting a good ducking

How would you like it if you spent most of your life eating bread? My diet seems to consist of stale and inedible pieces. I would prefer it if you threw me handfuls of river plants and small freshwater creatures, but it's probably easier if I forage for them myself.

A Mallard duck

I am a Mallard duck, so naturally I'm an expert on rivers. You might have the idea that my life is becoming increasingly unpleasant. Most people think that the amount of <u>pollution</u>, litter, industry, roads, housing and leisure facilities found along the UK's rivers would be ruining the environment. However, a recent national survey on the quality of the UK's rivers by the <u>Environment Agency</u> has painted a different picture.

The amount of grass, bushes and trees growing along the banks of rivers has increased in the last ten years. The <u>habitat</u> for ducks and small mammals has actually improved.

The survey also counted the number of <u>aquatic macro-invertebrates</u> (water bugs) found in each river. This showed that most of the rivers in the UK are clean. Less than a quarter scored below satisfactory for water quality, the survey also discovered that water quality has improved in over three-quarters of the UK's rivers. This is great news for us ducks.

Three cheers for the Environment Agency, who is responsible for the quality of the rivers and streams in the UK. Pollution from farming and industry is tightly controlled, with frequent visits from inspectors. Waste from sewage works has been significantly reduced and water companies have been given more responsibility for keeping rivers clean.

So, next time you are standing on a riverbank, about to throw me a morsel of the doughy stuff, spare a thought for my environment, and give yourself a pat on the back that things are actually getting better.

⬆ There are approximately 64 000 hectares of running water in the UK.

➡ The global population of mallard ducks is 17.5 million, in the UK there are 115 000 pairs of mallard ducks.

⬇ Fertiliser from farmers' fields is helping river bank plants to grow.

⬆ Aquatic macro-invertebrates include snails, worms, leeches, shrimps, mayflies, dragonflies, water bugs, beetles, caddis flies and midges. Their presence in rivers is an accurate indicator of the water quality.

⬆ 23% of UK rivers are judged as very good quality, 31% good, 23% satisfactory, 20% unsatisfactory and only 3% as truly bad.

➡ Currently 93% of rivers in England are classed as in good or fair condition for chemical content, compared with 73% in 1990. The levels of oxygen have also risen: 95% are of good or fair quality compared with 89% in 1990.

All of these are good indications of the health of a river

A river suffering from algae caused by nitrate pollution

EXAMINER'S TOP TIP

Even though the quality of the UK's rivers is improving, some rivers still suffer from nitrate pollution. This is caused by fertilisers being washed from farmers' fields into the water. The nitrates cause weeds and algae to grow, which can take over the river, block out sunlight and cause the water life to die.

A radical detox programme

I have an entry in the Guinness Book of Records. My name isn't mentioned, and I would never reveal my identity. Some people would hate me for what I did, but I think that if it hadn't been for me, the **River Rhine** would still be in the state that it was on the first of November 1986.

I'm responsible for the worst river pollution incident ever recorded. No one except me knows the exact cause of the fire that swept through the warehouse of Sandoz, one of Switzerland's major chemical companies. The warehouse was in the city of Basle, on the bank of the River Rhine.

The fire didn't do much damage to the river. It was the water used to put out the fire that did. The river life didn't stand a chance. The toxic slick stretched for 80 km, it took just less than two weeks to travel the 1000 km from Basle to the North Sea. All river life was killed up to 100 miles downstream from Basle. Scientists at the time said it would take at least 20 years for life to return.

The Rhine at Basle

The catastrophe led the International Commission for the Protection of the Rhine (ICPR) to create the Rhine Action Plan for Ecological Rehabilitation in 1987. The plan was to impose strict pollution controls along the length of the river, with the aim to make the Rhine clean again. The target was to see the return of salmon, which had been absent for almost 30 years.

Since the fire, the Rhine has been transformed. Thirty-seven species of fish can now be found in the river. In 1990 salmon returned to some of the Rhine's tributaries; 10 000–20 000 salmon now swim in the Rhine river basin.

People today stroll along the banks of the Rhine at Basle. They fish, swim, row and simply enjoy the river, in a way that would have been unimaginable in the 1980s. I like to think that I played my part in making that happen, at least, perhaps things would have been different if I hadn't taken that cigarette break over 20 years ago.

- A hundred years ago the Rhine was relatively clean. It supported a population of approximately 500 000 salmon along with 50 other species of fish.

- Since then the growth of settlements and industry along the course of the Rhine had turned the Rhine into one of the most polluted rivers in Europe. In 1958 the last salmon was caught, and by the end of the 21st century the Rhine contained less than 29 species of fish and was called the 'sewer of Europe'.

KEY FACTS

- The source of the Rhine is the Rheinwaldhorn Glacier, 3353 m above sea level in the Swiss Alps.

- The Rhine is 1320 km long, with a drainage basin of 185 000 km^2

- 50 million people live in the Rhine basin.

- The mouth of the Rhine is at Rotterdam, on the North Sea.

- The Rhine is Europe's longest river, passing through Switzerland, Germany and the Netherlands.

- Every second the Rhine discharges 2200 m^3 of water; over a year that adds up to 69 300 billion litres.

- Most of the landscape that the Rhine flows through is farmland and forest; however, just over 10% is built up area.

- On fifth of the world's chemicals are produced on the banks of the Rhine.

- The Rhine is the world's busiest waterway; barges carry coal, coke, grain, timber, iron ore and, of course, chemicals.

- During the fire 10 000–15 000 m^3 of water was washed into the river. The water carried with it 30 tonnes of chemicals including pesticides, herbicides, fungicides, dyes and mercury. This resulted in the deaths of 500 000 fish, 220 tonnes of eels and a total of 400 km of river wiped of life.

- Monitoring stations have been built along the Rhine, to check the quality of the water every six minutes, 24 hours a day. Polluters can be traced quickly and fined.

EXAMINER'S TOP TIPS

Pollution can have short-term and long-term effects. The short-term effect of the pollution from Basle was the immediate death of the fish, eels and other river life. The long-term effect was that it was going to take about 20 years for the river to recover from the disaster.

National (car) Parks

It was one of those family outings from Hell. August Bank Holiday Monday, one of the hottest summers on record, and my parents had the brilliant idea of a day trip to the Peak District. They loaded me and my brother into the back of our people carrier (the model without air conditioning), and we were off.

It was an hour down the motorway, which was a relatively short drive, but long enough for the arguments to begin. Dad wanted to head straight for Castleton – he had heard that there were some caves to visit around there - he fancied himself as an amateur speleologist (that's someone who likes to explore caves!), and was desperate to try out his new digital camera underground. He was quickly over-ruled by my mother, who said firmly that it was her day out, and she wanted to walk along the tranquil waters of the River Dove at Dovedale.

'Boring!' my brother yelled. He wanted to go to Stanage Edge, to go rock climbing. What was the point of visiting somewhere outdoors, if you were just going to walk about and look at things? He had a point, but no one else was desperate to attach ropes to various parts of their anatomy and spend the day clinging on to jagged rocks in terror of plummeting to their deaths.

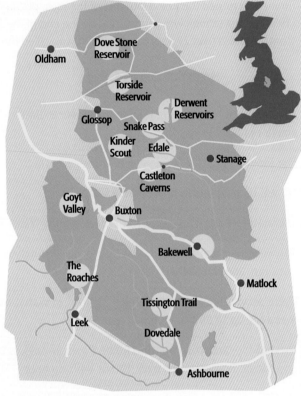

The Peak District National Park

I wanted to go sailing. I'd just read Ellen MacArthur's autobiography, and I was keen to take a dinghy onto Derwent Reservoir. No one asked my opinion. In the end Mum decided on a morning *watching* the rock climbing at Stanage, then an afternoon spent relaxing by the river Dove. Dad drove on in grim silence, trying to hide his cave disappointment.

As it turned out, lots of other families had had the very same idea. We hit our first traffic jam just outside Bakewell...

National Parks were designed to have a dual role: to provide a place for people to enjoy the outdoors, and to protect the environment.

Unfortunately, the dual role often leads to conflict between tourists who want to visit the national parks, and conservationists who want to prevent the landscape and wildlife from being damaged.

KEY FACTS

⬅ The Peak District was the UK's first <u>National Park</u>, designated in 1951.

➡ It is the second most visited National Park in the World, with 30 million visits a year.

⬇ The resident population of the Peak District is only 38 000.

⬆ In a summer week, on average, 500 000 people head for the Peak District.

⬅ 87% of visitors to the Peak District get there by car.

⬅ The Peak District is one out of 11 National Parks in the UK.

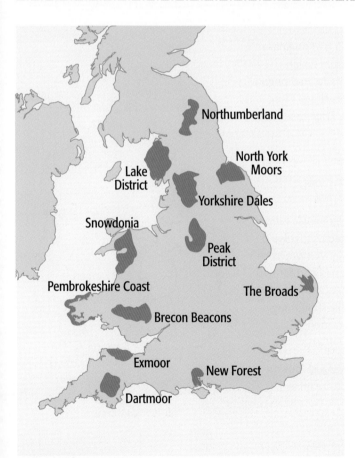

The UK's National Parks

On rocky ground

We made it to Stanage Edge around about lunchtime. The place was full of people: climbers, walkers, cyclists, horse riders and people picnicking. 'What do you expect, when the Peak District is less than 10 km from Sheffield, the UK's fifth largest city?' said my Dad, with a hint of smugness in his voice.

We carried our picnic onto the moorland, keeping a respectable distance from the hundreds of other families, and tucked into our sandwiches.

Stanage Edge

Dad pulled out his guide to the geology of the Peak District. The landscape is 50 million years old, he told us. It had originally been a vast river delta. The gritstone and shales from which Stanage Edge and the land underneath us were made, had begun life as sand and mud washed down by glacial meltwaters. They were laid down in layers, which was why Stanage Edge resembled an enormous pile of grey building blocks.

The rocks are impermeable, which means they don't allow water through. This also explained why we were getting soggy bottoms from the marshy water seeping through our picnic rug.

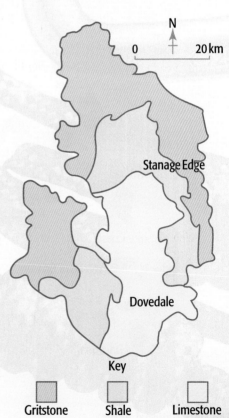

It was time to move on. Mum was keen to get to Dovedale before the best of the day had gone. Dad merrily informed us that we'd actually be travelling 300 million years back in time. We would be entering an area of carboniferous limestone. This had had formed long before the shale and gritstone, when the Peak District had been at the bottom of a tropical sea. It sounded like something from Doctor Who to me, but Dad said that fossil evidence had confirmed it.

Mum didn't care how the place was made. She was just looking forward to her walk along the riverbank and an ice cream at Milldale.

Key

| Gritstone | Shale | Limestone |

Geological map of the Peak District

KEY FACTS

⬆ Stanage Edge receives half a million tourist visits a year.

➡ The area has been managed by the Peak District National Park Authority in a number of ways:

- The car park has been covered in a material called Gopla. It is a mesh made from recycled plastic. The mesh protects the ground surface while allowing grass to grow through it.

- Footpaths have been laid that run from the car park to the main tourist sites. These have been made out of stone slabs recycled from demolished mills.

- Rangers have been employed to manage the number of visitors to the area and to limit their effect on the environment.

EXAMINER'S TOP TIPS

Rocks can be divided into three types: igneous (formed from magma), sedimentary (formed from sand, silt or the shells of sea creatures) and metamorphic (rocks that have been re-formed underground as a result of heat and pressure). The Peak District is made from two different sedimentary rocks.

Oh, for the wings of a dove!

As we arrived at the car park in Dovedale, it was as if we had entered another part of the world. Not only was the landscape completely different, but we discovered that we had turned up at a world record attempt for the number of tourists squeezed into 3 km of scenic river.

We all agreed that the view from the car park was lovely. Honey-coloured stone buildings, a winding path down to the river Dove and a glimpse of the wooded banks of the river itself. We had plenty of time to study the scene as it took half an hour to wait for a space to become free.

As we paid for our parking, the weary <u>National Trust</u> volunteer told us that the 395 car park spaces had been full by 10.00 am and that it had been one-in-one-out since then.

We joined the procession of walkers along the bank. Mum said wistfully that there should be wrens and kingfishers flitting across the river, along with trout

The path by the side of the River Dove

gliding beneath. I had to admit that the atmosphere in the tranquil <u>limestone gorge</u> was infectious. As I gazed up past the rock formations to the blue sky above, it was almost possible to forget that you were there with hundreds of other people doing exactly the same thing.

We made it to Milldale just in time to buy our ice cream (they had run out of flakes by then). 'How could anyone live here?' asked my brother. 'All these people would drive me mad!'

'A fair point,' said Dad, 'but nearly 1000 people here rely on tourism for their jobs. Tourists spend £137 million a year in the Peak District. You just can't turn them away.'

'Well,' said my brother, crunching the last of his cornet, 'at £2.50 an ice cream I'm not surprised!'

KEY FACTS

⬆ On average, 8000 people visit the Dove Valley every summer Bank Holiday.

➡ Dovedale is known as a <u>honeypot site</u>; that is, a location in a tourist area that becomes the focus for visitors.

⬇ The main attractions along the Dove valley are Reynard's Cave, Tissington Spires, Lover's Leap, Lion's Head Rock, Thorpe Cloud and Ilam Rock.

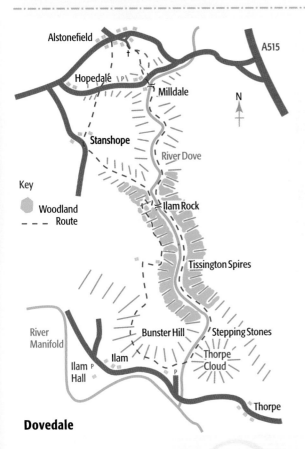

Dovedale

EXAMINER'S TOP TIPS

• Tourism can have positive and negative effects on a honeypot site.
• Positive effects include:

– Employment;
– Income for local businesses;
– Improvements in local facilities such as roads and amenities.

• Negative effects include:

– Jobs are often seasonal or part-time;
– House prices go up as people buy holiday homes;
– Roads become congested in peak times;
– The environment becomes damaged by pollution from vehicles, litter and footpath erosion.

Seeing in black and white

Allow me to introduce myself. I'm 70 cm tall and weigh about 5 kg. I'm black, apart from my chest, under my flippers and around my eyes, where I am white. I eat mainly fish and I get most of my water by eating snow. I look ridiculous on land, where I prefer to slide rather than waddle. However, I am a fabulous swimmer.

I hope you have worked out by now that I am a penguin, not a vertically challenged nun. I'm a type of penguin called an Adelie penguin. There are about eight million of us, we are mostly found in Antarctica and around the islands of the Southern Ocean.

Antarctica has remained untouched for over 160 million years. However, the number of tourists visiting the continent is growing, the potential for <u>mineral extraction</u> is becoming increasingly significant, and <u>global warming</u> is having disastrous consequences for this unique and fragile environment.

I've been doing my research and Antarctica is already relatively well protected. In 1959 the <u>Antarctic Treaty</u> was signed by 12 countries. The treaty included agreements on using the place for peaceful

An Adelie penguin

means, allowing scientists to work there and keeping Antarctica free from nuclear weapons and waste.

Since then the Convention for the Conservation of Antarctic Seals (CCAS) was signed in 1972, the Convention for the Conservation of Antarctic Marine Living Resources (CCAMLR) was signed in 1980 and the Environmental Protocol was passed in 1998 further protecting Antarctica from pollution and mining.

My environmentalist friends say that if Antarctica were to be become a <u>world park</u>, any human interference in the continent would be controlled more than it is now. At the moment Antarctica has no <u>world heritage sites</u>, no national parks and not even a <u>nature reserve</u>. Perhaps being a world park would make a difference and I would feel safe.

⬆ Antarctica is 1.5 times the size of the USA, and 50 times the size of the UK.

➡ It contains two thirds of the world's fresh water, however most of this is locked up in 91% of the world's ice.

⬇ It is the world's driest, coldest and windiest continent!

⬆ At times the temperature can fall to –50°C.

⬅ Antarctica plays a vital role maintaining the world's life-support systems, including the circulation of ocean currents and atmospheric systems.

➡ Seven countries claim territory there, although they have agreed not to become involved in conflict relating to territorial claims.

⬈ Antarctica has a fragile ecosystem, mainly because a lot of the marine life relies on krill, which is at the bottom of the food chain. If the number of krill was to decline, this could have knock-on effects on the other creatures that depend on krill for their survival.

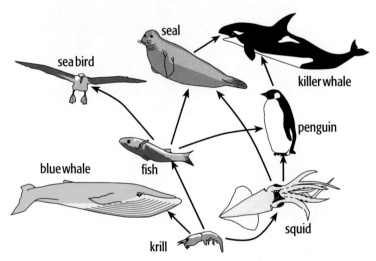

An Antartic food chain

EXAMINER'S TOP TIP

Antarctica is a good example of how a local action can have a global effect. Every time you switch a light on, a little extra fossil fuel gets being burnt in a power station nearby. That fossil fuel produces CO_2, which contributes to the greenhouse effect and raises world temperatures. As the temperatures rise, ice melts in Antarctica and the penguins are affected. Illuminating, isn't it?

Fish and ships

Sometimes I think to myself, what is all the fuss about? Only 2% of Antarctica is rock. That's important for a penguin, because we like to lay our eggs on solid ground, and ice has a habit of melting before the eggs hatch. But surely a gigantic lump of ice at the bottom of the world is of little value to a human?

Apparently Antarctica has valuable fish reserves. I suppose there is enough to go around, although I became worried when I found out that over 250 000 tonnes were caught last year.

Then there are the <u>natural resources</u>: oil (tens of billions of barrels), coal (11% of the world's reserves) and countless other minerals such as iron ore, copper, gold, nickel and platinum.

I've been told that 12 000 tourists a year come to Antarctica. There is an international association of Antarctic tour operators, who follow strict codes to prevent damage to the environment. As a penguin I don't mind the tourists, as they tend to leave us alone.

Another worry is conflict between the nations who claim to have territorial rights over Antarctica. The problem is that a lot of the territories overlap. We penguins all remember the stories that were coming from the Falkland Islands during the war in the 1980s. There the troops used our cousin penguins for target practice – so we can't risk a repeat of that here.

As it is, life goes on in Antarctica, until someone decides how else the place should be protected. In reality it is not a threat from the continent that is making our lives a misery: the real damage is being done thousands of miles away.

Tourism in Antarctica

⬆ The Southern Ocean contains 110–150 million tonnes of krill that could be exploited for food.

➡ Argentina, Australia, Chile, France, New Zealand, Norway and the UK all claim territory in Antarctica.

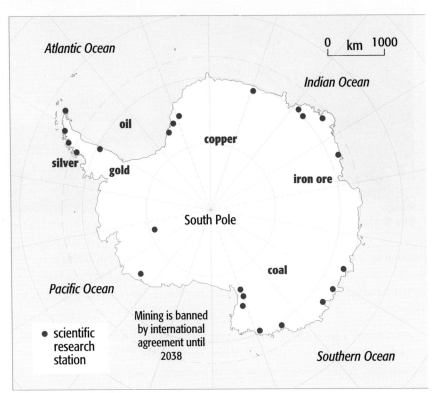

Atlantic Ocean

0 km 1000

Indian Ocean

oil

copper

silver

gold

iron ore

South Pole

coal

Pacific Ocean

• scientific research station

Mining is banned by international agreement until 2038

Southern Ocean

Antarctica's resources

EXAMINER'S TOP TIPS

Antarctica is one of the last places left on earth that is relatively untouched by human development. This gives it a unique value for researchers and conservationists.

Meltdown!

This year, a 115 km-long iceberg broke off from Antarctica, floated along the coast, and crashed into a glacier called the Drygalski ice tongue. The iceberg, called B-15A, did not do any damage, but it blocked off the route from a penguin nesting site to the sea.

This made the journey from the nesting site to the sea so long that the chicks would have died from starvation before their mothers completed the journey to collect food. Fortunately, the iceberg continued to move, so the route was not blocked for long.

The iceberg   **The Drygalski ice tongue**

The B-15A iceberg

It is evidence that Antarctica is cracking up. Many blame human activity. In the last 50 years the average temperature in Antarctica has risen by 2.5°C. This matches an increase in the level of atmospheric Carbon Dioxide (CO_2), which has risen by a third in the same time. The extra carbon dioxide increases the greenhouse effect, and the continent warms up.

Parts of the ice shelves that surround Antarctica are splitting and breaking away. Whole islands that used to be ringed by ice are now completely ice-free. Penguins may have to find new nesting sites. Old nesting sites may become inaccessible due to ice movements, or unsuitable because global warming is causing more snow to fall, and we can't lay our eggs on snow.

I have decided to write to George W. Bush. In the same year that the iceberg crashed into the penguin colony, 141 countries, accounting for 55% of the world's greenhouse gas emissions, ratified (gave formal approval to) the Kyoto Protocol. This is a pledge to cut greenhouse gas emissions by 5.2% by 2012. That gives us Antarctic dwellers hope, but it is relatively worthless until the world's top polluter – the US – signs up.

If something isn't done soon, we'll all be able to swim right up to the White House and tell the President exactly what we think of his environmental policies.

White House
14,344 km

⬆ Adelie penguins pair for life.

➡ Adelie nesting sites can be 30–100 km from the sea. This prevents the sites from being flooded, but it is a long walk for a penguin to reach them.

⬇ Global warming is also causing seals to relocate, which is bad news for penguins, as the seals are moving closer to the nesting sites.

⬆ If Antarctic temperatures were to double, scientists predict that ice sheets the size of Spain would break off and eventually disappear into the sea.

⬆ Global warming happens when there is an increase in the amount of carbon dioxide (CO_2) in the earth's atmosphere. CO_2 has the effect of trapping heat that is radiated from the surface of the earth. This causes the temperature of the planet to increase.

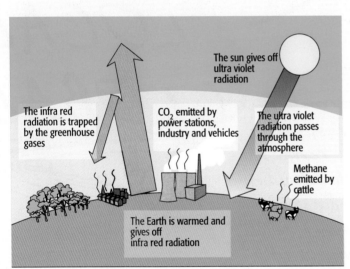

The sun gives off ultra violet radiation

The infra red radiation is trapped by the greenhouse gases

CO_2 emitted by power stations, industry and vehicles

The ultra violet radiation passes through the atmosphere

Methane emitted by cattle

The Earth is warmed and gives off infra red radiation

The Greenhouse effect

EXAMINER'S TOP TIP

• Everything is delicately balanced in Antarctica. It is very difficult to predict how changing an apparently small feature could affect the rest of the continent.

• Antarctica plays a vital role in controlling the earth's atmosphere and ocean currents. If global warming causes the widespread melting of the continent's ice, this could have devastating consequences for global weather patterns and climatic conditions.

Tourists erode footpaths, drop litter, overcrowd places, and pollute with car fumes.

Tourist developments destroy habitats, spoil views, pollute air and water and create waste.

ACTIONS

Farmers remove hedgerows, disturb nesting sites and pollute waterways with chemicals.

Global warming is caused by carbon dioxide from burning fossil fuels trapping heat in the earth's atmosphere.

The Rhine was polluted with 15,000 m3 water containing 30 tonnes of toxic chemicals.

LOCAL

GLOBAL

National Park status protects the Peak District from overdevelopment.

Information centres, car parks, rangers, footpath rebuilding and education programmes reduce the impact of tourism.

Water quality in the Rhine is monitored daily. Detected pollution is stopped.

MANAGEMENT

Antarctica is protected by several international treaties. There is a possibility that it could become a World Park.

The EU now pays farmers to protect the environment of their farms.

The Environment Agency sets strict laws and penalties to prevent people polluting rivers in the UK.

Honeypot sites become overrun by tourists and the environment spoilt.

Local people cannot find jobs outside the tourist season, house prices become too high and the area becomes spoilt.

Global warming is melting Antarctica, affecting penguins and having unknown consequences for the earth's atmosphere.

EFFECTS

400 km of the Rhine was wiped of life. 500,000 fish were killed and 220 tonnes of eels died.

ACTIONS AND EFFECTS

Fertilisers cause weeds and algae to grow so that waterways become choked and lifeless.

Tourism earns the Peak District £737 million a year and employs 1000 people.

75% of the UK's rivers are clean.

RESULTS

Antarctica's treaties prevent development, conflict and the exploitation of Antarctica's resources and wildlife

The Rhine now has 37 species of fish and salmon are returning to the river.

The Kyoto Accord is an international commitment to reduce significantly carbon dioxide emissions to prevent global warming.

Test your knowledge 4

1 Complete the crossword using the clues below. Each word is a source of river pollution.

a)
b)
c)
d)
e)
f)
g)
h)
i)

The crossword spells vertically: P O L L U T I O N

a) Used by farmers to kill bugs.
b) Built to improve transport connections.
c) Dropped by thoughtless people.
d) Used by farmers to improve their yields.
e) Manufacturing.
f) Unwanted material, e.g. sewage.
g) Activities undertaken in free time.
h) Provides a place to live.
i) Chemicals used by farmers to help plants to grow.

(9 marks)

2 Decide whether these statements about the quality of the UK's rivers are true of false.

a) There are 64 000 hectares of running water in the UK.
b) 75% of the UK's rivers suffer from poor water quality.
c) The quality of water in the majority of the UK's rivers is improving.
d) Habitats for wildlife along river banks are being destroyed at an ever-increasing rate.

(4 marks)

3 Match the facts and figures about the Rhine to the correct statement (remember to add the units).

a) Length   500 000
b) Drainage basin area   400
c) Discharge in seconds   1958
d) Number of salmon in the Rhine 100 years ago 2200^3
e) Date that the last salmon was caught   185 000
f) Number of fish killed in 1986   1320
g) Length of the river wiped of life   500 000

(7 marks)

4 Describe the action that has been taken to clean up the Rhine and prevent further pollution.

(4 marks)

5 Label the key places on the blank map of the Peak District.

Choose from

a) Kinder Scout
b) Castleton Caverns
c) Derwent Reservoir
d) Stanage Edge
e) Bakewell
f) River Dove

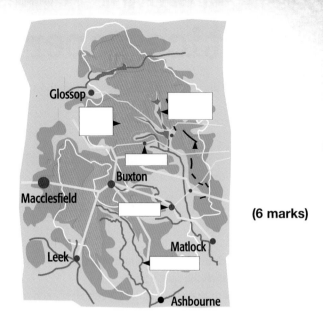

(6 marks)

6 Divide these descriptions into those that describe limestone and those that describe gritstone.

a) Impermeable.
b) Permeable.
c) Formed 300 million years ago.
d) Formed 50 million years ago.
e) Originally was under a tropical sea.
f) Originally was a river delta.
g) Hard and resistant to weathering.
h) Soft and dissolves in rain water.

(8 marks)

7 What are the benefits and problems of tourism in the Peak District? How can the problems be solved to reduce the impact of tourism on local people and the environment?

(6 marks)

8 Fill in the gaps in the paragraph below to describe Antarctica.

Antarctica is .... times the size of the UK. It contains two thirds of the world's .... and it plays a crucial role in managing the earth's .... Only 2% of Antarctica is ...., the rest is .... Temperatures can fall to as low as –50°C. Antarctica has a fragile ....; affecting one part could have a disastrous effect on the whole. At the bottom of the food chain is ....; this tiny shrimp-like creature is vital to the survival of much larger mammals higher up the food chain, such as leopard seals and ....

ecosystem   climate   ice   killer whales

50   rock   krill   fresh water

(8 marks)

9 Why is Antarctica threatened?

(4 marks)

10 Should Antarctica be made into a World Park?

(6 marks)
(Total 62 marks)

Practice paper

Write your name and the name of your school in the spaces below.

First name ....

Last name ....

School ....

Remember
- The test is half an hour long.
- You will need: pen, pencil, rubber and ruler.
- Try to answer all the questions.
- The number of marks available is given after each question.
- Check your work carefully.

1 a) The diagram below shows the formation of the Himalayas mountain range.

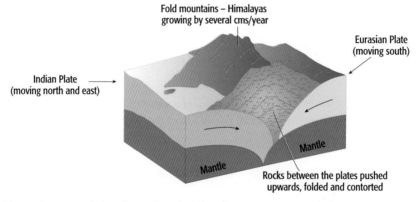

Name the type of plate boundary that the diagram represents.

....

(1 mark)

b) Composite volcanoes are characterised by being steep sided and having explosive eruptions.

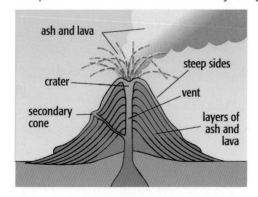

Explain the causes of **one** of these characteristics.

....

(1 mark)

84

c) The map below shows the pattern of the eruptions of the Soufriere volcano on the Island of Montserrat between 1995–97.

Suggest **two** reasons why the impact of a volcanic eruption may be more severe in an LEDC than in an MEDC.

Reason 1: ....

....

....

Reason 2: ....

....

....

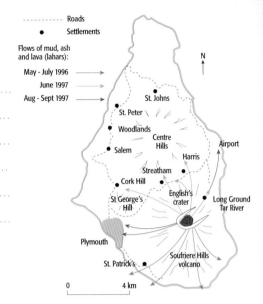

2 The Indian Ocean tsunami that killed almost 300 000 people on Boxing Day in 2004 has been described as one of the world's worst natural disasters.

The map below shows the time after the earthquake that the tsunami waves took to reach the countries affected.

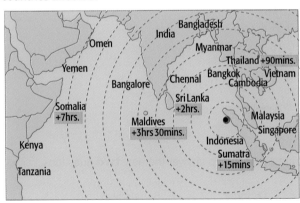

a) How long did it take the tsunami waves to reach Thailand?
    Tick the correct box.

    ½ hour ☐   1 hour ☐   1 ½ hours ☐   2 hours ☐

    (1 mark)

b) People in Thailand described the sea 'drawing back' from the coast before the wave struck.

    Why did this phenomenon happen?

    ....

    (1 mark)

c) How could the number of people killed be reduced if a tsunami were to happen in this region in the future?

....

(1 mark)

3 a) Use an answer from the list below to fill in the gap in the sentence.

HDI   **Adult Literacy**   **Life Expectancy**   **GDP**

Malawi in East Africa has been identified as an LEDC because it has a low ...., which is an

indicator of development that combines measures of health, wealth and education in a country.

(1 mark)

b) Give **one** reason why the average calorific intake in LEDCs is a lot lower than MEDCs.

....

....

(1 mark)

4 The map below shows the country of origin of a sample of clothes from an average Year 9 class.

a) Give the letter of the country from the list of countries below to answer the next **two** questions.

A. China   **B.** UK   **C.** USA   **D.** India   **E.** Bangladesh

(i) The LEDC country that manufactured the largest number of clothes is ....

(1 mark)

(ii) The MEDC country that manufactured the largest number of clothes is ....

(1 mark)

b) Suggest **one** reason why clothes manufacturers are choosing to locate their factories in Eastern Europe and South East Asia.

....

(1 mark)

c) Describe the conditions that you might expect to find workers experiencing in some of these clothing factories.

....

....

(1 mark)

5 a) LEDC's that make most of their money by exporting just one crop are described as being **over dependent** on that crop.

Suggest **one** reason why over dependence on a crop could lead to problems for a country in the future.

....

....

(1 mark)

b) **Fair trade** is a system designed to improve the income and quality of life for farmers in LEDCs.

Describe **one** way that fair trade achieves this.

....

....

(1 mark)

6 The Tour de France is a world famous cycle race that happens every summer.

a) Why will the cyclists find the stages of the race in the southern half of France a lot **harder** than the stages in the northern half of France?

....

(1 mark)

b) Which river will the cyclists cross between Miramas and Montpellier in the South of France?
Tick the correct box.

Seine ☐   Garonne ☐   Loire ☐   Rhône ☐

(1 mark)

7 The graph below shows the changes in the employment structure in France over the last 50 years.

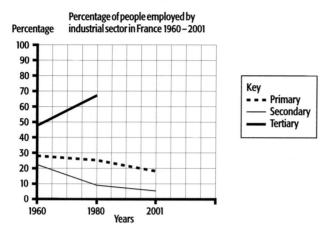

Percentage of people employed by industrial sector in France 1960–2001

a) In 2001 the percentage of people employed in the tertiary sector was 77%. Complete the graph by plotting this figure in the correct place.

(1 mark)

b) Suggest one reason why employment in manufacturing in France has declined between 1960 and 2001.

....

(1 mark)

8 The diagram below shows the countries from which the 77 million tourists who visit France each year come.

The origin of tourists who come to France

Italy 9%
Belgium & Luxembourg 12%
Netherlands 16%
UK & Ireland 16%
Germany 21%
Other 26%

0   10   20   30   40
% of total arrivals

a) Which **two** countries from the diagram **do not** have a land border with France? Choose your answer from the list below.

Germany   UK   Netherlands

Belgium   Luxembourg   Italy

.... and ....

(1 mark)

b) Many of the regions in France have invested a lot of money developing their tourist industry. Name a region and describe one tourist attraction that the region has.

Region: ....

(1 mark)

Tourist attraction: ....

(1 mark)

9 The diagram shows a selection of creatures that you could find in or near a river in the UK.

a)   b)   c)   d)   e)

a) Give the letter of the creature that is most likely to be used by scientists to measure the water quality of a river.

....

(1 mark)

b) Salmon are only found in rivers where the water quality is very good. Suggest one action that a water authority can take to encourage salmon to return to a previously polluted river.

....

....

(1 mark)

10 The diagram below is a summary of the causes of global warming.

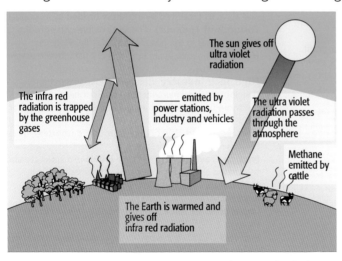

The sun gives off ultra violet radiation

The infra red radiation is trapped by the greenhouse gases

_____ emitted by power stations, industry and vehicles

The ultra violet radiation passes through the atmosphere

Methane emitted by cattle

The Earth is warmed and gives off infra red radiation

a) Write on the missing label, choosing it from the list below.

Sulphur Dioxide   Carbon Dioxide   Ozone   Carbon Monoxide

(1 mark)

b) Global warming is having an impact on Antarctica, which could cause problems for the local and the global environment.

Describe either a local or a global problem caused by global warming affecting Antarctica.

....

(1 mark)

(Total 26 marks)

Glossary

Active volcano A volcano that has erupted recently, is currently erupting, or is expected to erupt again.

Adult literacy The percentage of people over the age of 18 who can read or write in a particular country.

Agriculture The use of land to grow crops and rear animals to provide food and other products.

Aid A transfer of resources such as money, food and skills from one area to another, in order to provide some sort of help.

Antarctic Treaty An agreement between countries to protect Antarctica and not to perform certain activities there, such as weapons testing.

Antiretroviral A type of drug designed to prevent the HIV virus from attacking the immune system.

Aquatic macro-invertebrates Small water creatures.

Basic/Basaltic lava A runny type of lava that contains a low amount Silica (less than 52%).

Branch plants Factories belonging to a TNC located away from the headquarters, usually abroad in LEDCs.

Carboniferous limestone A type of limestone formed 300 million years ago during tropical conditions.

Cash crops Agricultural products that are sold for profit; usually by LEDCs as exports.

Coast Land which is next to the sea.

Collision boundary Where two continental plates are pushing together.

Colony A territory occupied and governed by settlers from another country.

Commercial farming Farming to sell produce for profit.

Composite (strato) volcanoes Steep sided volcanoes found at destructive plate boundaries, formed from sticky lava, resulting in explosive eruptions.

Conchyliculture Farming oysters and mussels.

Conservative boundary Where two tectonic plates are sliding past each other.

Constructive boundary Where two tectonic plates are moving apart from each other.

Continental crust The tectonic plates that form land; they are thicker and lighter than oceanic crust.

Crust Hard rock forming the outer layer of the Earth.

Cryptodome Bulge on the side of Mt St Helens in the USA, formed before the eruption in 1980.

Deindustrialisation A decline in manufacturing employment in a particular place.

Delta A landform created by deposition at the mouth of river.

Destructive boundary Where continental and oceanic plates collide.

Development Improvements in standards of living and quality of life that follow from a country becoming wealthier.

Dormant volcano A volcano that has not erupted recently, which may erupt one day in the future.

Environment Agency Government organisation responsible for protecting rivers and lakes in the UK.

Epicentre The point on the ground surface directly above the place underground where an earthquake began.

Eruption An event where molten rock forces its way to the Earth's surface and is released by a volcano or through cracks in the ground.

Estuary The tidal part of a river.

European Union (EU) A trade bloc formed by some countries in Europe involving the free movement of people, goods and services between member states.

Exclusion zone An area surrounding an active volcano that is out of bounds for safety reasons.

Exports Goods and services that are sold abroad.

Extinct volcano A volcano that is never expected to erupt again.

Fair trade A system of trade where producers in LEDCs are paid a price for their goods, which enables them to achieve an acceptable standard of living.

Faults Splits or breaks in the Earth's crust; either following the path of a plate boundary, or found anywhere on a plate.

Gendarmerie The French police force.

Glacier A river of ice that flows from highland areas to lowland areas.

Global warming An increase in the world's temperature as a result of the pollution in the atmosphere.

Globalisation The spread of economic activity worldwide increasing links between countries.

Gorge Steep sided river valley caused by the retreat of a waterfall, or the roof of a cave collapsing.

Greenhouse effect The action of gases in the earth's atmosphere trapping heat radiated from the earth's surface, which causes global temperatures to rise.

Gritstone A coarse sandstone, often used for millstones or grinding wheels.

Gross Domestic Product (GDP) The total value of goods and services produced by a country divided by its population.

Groundnut (peanut) The small edible underground tubers of a vegetable in the pea and bean family of plants.

Habitat The immediate environment used by a creature to meet its needs.

High Tech industry Companies involved in the development and manufacture of electronics, computer hardware or software, pharmaceuticals, biotechnology or telecommunications.

Honeypot site A very popular tourist destination, usually a scenic village or beauty spot.

Human Development Index (HDI) An index created by the United Nations to measure development.

Ice shelves Thick masses of ice that are permanently attached to land but which project out to sea.

Impermeable Rock that does not allow water to pass through it.

Imports Goods and services that are bought from abroad.

Independence Freedom from control by another country, e.g. a colonial power.

International Monetary Fund (IMF) A financial institution created in 1945 to help countries to trade more freely with each other.

Kyoto Protocol An agreement between countries to reduce the amount of greenhouse gases that are emitted by industrialised nations.

Lahar A combination of ash and water forming an unstoppable flow of dense, hot slurry.

Lava Magma that flows over the ground surface.

Less Economically Developed Country (LEDC) Poorer countries of the world that tend to have a low standard of living and quality of life.

Life expectancy The average number of years that people live. It can be calculated for a country or a group of people.

Limestone A type of sedimentary rock formed from calcium carbonate obtained from the remains of sea creatures.

Magma Semi-solid molten rock found beneath the Earth's crust, forming the mantle.

Malnourishment Lack of adequate nutrition resulting from an unbalanced diet or an insufficiency of particular vitamins and minerals.

Mantle The thickest layer of the Earth, consisting of semi-solid molten rock, found beneath the crust.

Manure Animal excreta mixed with straw or chemical fertilizer that is used to fertilize land.

Migrate To go from one region, country or place of abode to settle in another, often in a foreign country.

Mineral extraction The removal of natural resources from the earth by mining or quarrying.

Moorland An area of open land consisting of damp peaty soil colonised by grasses, heathers, bracken and moss.

More Economically Developed Country (MEDC) Richer countries of the world, which tend to have a high standard of living and quality of life.

Multicultural A society with prominent characteristics of several cultural groups or peoples.

Multinational company A company with interests in more than one country.

National Park An area of land set aside by the state to provide enjoyment and environmental protection.

National Trust A charity that owns and conserves historic buildings and areas of outstanding natural beauty in the UK.

Natural resources Raw materials that are provided by the physical environment.

Nature reserve An area of land with a high level of environmental protection and controls.

New towns Towns that have been planned and built from scratch.

New World Former colonies, such as Australia, New Zealand, South Africa and the USA.

Nutrients Minerals that provide nourishment to plants and animals.

Obesity Overweight by 30 % of the ideal body weight.

Oceanic crust The tectonic plates that form the sea beds; they are thinner and heavier than continental crust.

Plate boundaries The point where two tectonic plates meet.

Pollution The introduction of anything into the environment that could cause harm or damage.

Primary effect An effect that is caused directly by a natural hazard.

Primary industry The extraction of natural resources from the environment.

Pyroclastic flows Avalanches of burning gases, ash and red-hot rocks that explode from the eruptions of composite volcanoes.

Recession Slowing or declining economic growth.

Regeneration The renewal of an area by investment and rebuilding.

Regional aid Money provided by governments to help depressed areas to regenerate.

Reindustrialisation The return of industry and employment to areas that have previously suffered from deindustrialisation.

RER Réseau Express Régional – a regional express train network linking the surrounding areas of Paris to the centre of the city.

Richter scale A measure of the energy released by an earthquake; measured from 1–10, with each point being ten times the magnitude of the previous point. Developed by Charles Richter in 1935.

Runoff Rainwater that flows over the surface of the ground.

Secondary effect An effect that follows indirectly from a natural hazard.

Secondary industry Manufacturing, that turns raw materials into finished products.

Seismic waves Shock waves produced by an earthquake.

Seismometers Instrument designed to measure the shock waves produced by an earthquake.

Seismophobia The fear of earthquakes.

Services Activities that meet people's needs, such as retail, health and education.

Shale A sedimentary rock made from layers of compressed clay.

Shield volcanoes Gentle sided volcanoes found at constructive plate boundaries, formed from runny lava, resulting in non-explosive eruptions.

Silica Mineral element, actually Silicon dioxide (SiO_2), found in sand, quartz and granite.

SONACOS State-run peanut oil company in Senegal.

Strain gauge Instrument designed to measure movement between two objects; in this case, tectonic plates.

Strato (composite) volcano Steep sided volcanoes found at destructive plate boundaries, formed from sticky lava, resulting in explosive eruptions.

Subsidiaries Factories or offices belonging to a TNC located away from the headquarters, usually abroad in LEDCs.

Subsistence farming Farming that provides food for the farmer's own family rather than for selling.

Sustainable development Economic growth that enables the needs of the present generation to be met without compromising the ability to meet the needs of future generations.

Tectonic plates A large, rigid section of the Earth's crust.

Tertiarisation The growth of the service sector, usually as a result of deindustrialisation.

Tertiary industry Services, such as education, health, retail and leisure/tourism.

TGV Train à Grande Vitesse – the high speed train operated by SNCF, the rail network in France.

Tilt/creep/gravity meters A variety of instruments used to detect movement on the Earth's surface.

Trade surplus The condition when a country makes more money from its exports than it spends on its imports.

Traditional manufacturing Manufacturing that involves iron and steel, rail, ship building and vehicles. Also the textiles industry.

Transnational Company (TNC) A company with interests in more than one country.

Tsunami A tidal wave created by an earthquake under the sea.

United Nations (UN) International organisation created in 1945 to promote peace, international cooperation and security.

Volcanic bombs Rocks and boulders ejected during a volcanic eruption.

Volcanoes Cone-shaped mountains that have been formed by magma being forced onto the Earth's surface.

Vulcanologist A scientist who studies volcanoes.

World Bank Financial organisation created in 1945 to provide loans for countries to assist in economic development.

World heritage site A global site of cultural or natural significance that has been identified for special protection.

World park An area of global importance that has been set aside for special protection.

World trade Trade in goods and services across the globe.

World Trade Organisation (WTO) Organisation established to promote free trade between countries around the globe.

Answers to test your knowledge questions

Test your knowledge 1
Volcanoes and earthquakes

1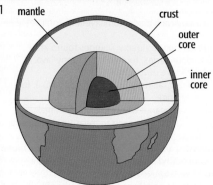
mantle, crust, outer core, inner core

2 Pacific plate

3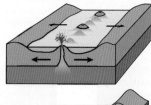
a) Constructive

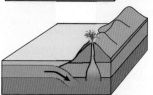
b) Destructive

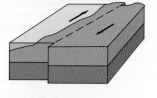
c) Conservative

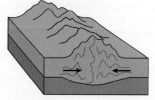
d) Collision

4 Mt Etna – composite, sticky lava, pyroclastic flows; Mauna Loa – shield, runny lava, gentle eruption.

5 Pyroclastic flows – travel at up to 200 km/hour; can reach temperatures of 1000°C; are made from dust, ash and rocks (some as big as houses), will incinerate anything they touch, will melt glass, happen when composite volcanoes erupt.

6 The Juan de Fuca plate is moving towards the North American plate at a rate of a few **millimetres** a year. The **Juan de Fuca** plate was being pushed under the **North American** plate because it was an oceanic plate, which made it the heavier of the two. As the Juan de Fuca plate was being pushed into the **mantle**, it melted and extra **magma** was produced. The molten rock was thick and sticky because it was mixed with **sediments** from the Pacific Ocean. This extra magma increased the **pressure** underground, so it pushed to the surface. Once inside Mt St Helens the path of the lava was blocked by **solidified** lava from previous eruptions. Eventually the pressure inside the volcano became so great that the mountain literally **exploded**.

7 43 832 were killed; most on the east coast; the waves arrived peak first so there was no warning; the waves curved around the island and travelled up the west coast; hotels were flooded; trains were ripped off their lines; the waves were six metres high in some places; people lost their loved ones, homes, possessions and jobs.

8 • The Indo-Australian plate was moving underneath the Eurasian plate.
   • Pressure built up along the fault line between the two plates.
   • The pressure was released when the Eurasian plate 'flicked' upwards.
   • The shockwave caused by the earthquake sent waves travelling away from the fault at speeds of 500 km/hour.
   • As the waves reached the coast, the bottom of the wave was slowed by friction, while the top of the wave continued to travel at high speed.
   • The front of the wave reared up, then came crashing down onto the coast.
   • The waves had such long wave lengths that they did not break when they hit the shore. Instead, they continued to flow inland for several miles.

9 Your answer should include: lack of prediction/warning; inadequate evacuation procedures; most buildings don't have the latest

earthquake proof designs, insufficient resources for emergency services. It should also include examples from the earthquakes and volcanoes described in the double pages.

10 Your answer should include: the economic benefits of living near a volcano, tourism and farming; farmland is fertile near to volcanoes because eruptions leave minerals and nutrients on the slopes of the volcano; people may have inherited land/property that was developed at a time when the hazard was not active; people take a risk between the benefits and possible consequences; the probability of experiencing an eruption or earthquake is less than the advantages of living in a particular location. It should also include examples from the double pages.

Test your knowledge 2
Development

1 a) = (iii), b) = (iv), c) = (ii), d) = (v), e) = (i), f) = (vi).

2 a) = 75 years, b) = 165th, c) = 38 years, d) = $570 per person, e) = 60%, f) = 85%.

3 MEDCs = heart disease, obesity, high blood pressure and waste; LEDCs = malnourishment, hunger, being underweight, starvation.

4 Some people in LEDCs are **subsistence** farmers. This means that they grow their own food. If there is a **drought** or their crops are attacked by disease or **pests**, they may not be able to grow enough to meet their needs. A lot of the best farm land in LEDCs has been bought by **TNCs** or the national government, to be farmed for **cash crops**. This creates **money** for the economy, but results in people having to farm on second-rate land that does not grow as much **food**. If the price of cash crops **falls** on the world market, commercial farmers in LEDCs will not make enough money to buy the food required to feed themselves or their families. Some LEDCs are involved in **civil wars** or other conflicts, which sometimes makes it impossible for some farmers to grow crops or raise animals.

5 Cotton = Benin; dye = Germany; pumice = Turkey; copper = Namibia; zinc = Australia.

6 For example, Benin = people work for 60p a day, long hours, hot sun, child labour; Germany = well paid, health and safety laws, secure jobs; Namibia = dangerous, long hours, hard work mining copper, arsenic poisoning, low pay.

7 Natural resources such as copper and zinc are only found in certain places. Raw materials such as cotton will only grow in particular climates. The cost of goods from some countries is less than for others, e.g. cotton from Benin versus cotton from the USA; the cost of labour is much cheaper in LEDCs than it is in MEDCs.

8 Similarities: low income; influence of IMF/World Bank; encouraged to adopt free trade; encouraged to promote ownership of businesses by individuals; affected by TNCs/world prices, both have experienced drought.
Differences: Senegal is affected by cheaper/subsidised foreign imports. Coffee sales in the world are booming; some coffee farmers are being helped by fair trade schemes.

9 Increased fairness through: paying a fair price for goods; making sure workers are paid a fair wage; health/safety regulations; laws controlling working hours/paid holiday/overtime; allowing countries to use trade barriers to protect their farmers/workers, allowing the governments of countries to support their farmers/workers.

10 Physical: LEDCs often suffer from extreme climatic conditions; their relief may make it hard to develop settlements and industry; they may have a lack of natural resources; they may be inaccessible/remote; there may be a lot of disease/predators.
Human: LEDCs may have war/conflicts which delay development, their governments may be corrupt or mismanage the economies, they may be in a system of trade which doesn't make the country any money (e.g. selling agricultural products, which are cheap, to buy manufactured products, which are expensive); they may have loans/debts that have to be paid, reducing the amount of money that is available for development. Many of these could be illustrated using examples from the double pages. Think of how many of the human factors MEDCs are responsible for.

Test your knowledge 3
France

1 a) Mt Blanc, b) Rhône, c) Seine, d) Pyrenees, e) Alps, f) Paris Basin, g) Atlantic, h) Mediterranean.

R	T	N	I	S	A	B	S	I	R	A	P	S	Z
A	H	P	L	O	Y	H	N	B	M	R	L	L	P
M	S	O	R	B	C	P	A	T	V	K	P	P	B
P	E	O	N	N	E	W	B	H	P	L	B	V	S
O	I	V	G	E	M	L	U	M	R	F	C	B	N
J	N	A	E	N	A	R	R	E	T	I	D	E	M
W	E	N	P	N	M	K	G	H	J	R	C	V	M
Y	I	N	C	P	C	I	T	N	A	L	T	A	C
R	P	Y	R	E	N	E	E	S	W	Q	Z	U	O

2 Primary, 5.2, The extraction of resources from the land or sea.
Secondary, 17.7, Manufacturing raw materials into products.
Tertiary, 77.1, Providing a service to people.

3 Traditional manufacturing in France, such as the manufacture of **iron and steel**, has lost jobs for three main reasons. People are buying manufactured goods from other countries, particularly from **newly industrialised countries** in SE Asia, rather than France. This is because those countries are able to produce similar products that are **better** and **cheaper**. Advances in technology have resulted in **machines** taking the place of **labour**. People are more skilled and educated in France, they prefer to work in the **service sector** or in research and development than in **manufacturing**. They may also be able to earn **higher** wages in these sectors.

4 Advantages: employment, culture and entertainment; a lot going on; connections to the rest of France/Europe/The world.
Disadvantages: congestion; pollution; expensive living costs; overcrowded.

5 Housing: built new towns/redeveloped areas with new housing. Employment: created many new jobs on the edge of Paris and in new developments such as La Défense.
Transport: built the Boulevard Péripherique, the RER and extended the TGV and the Métro.
Services: provided new schools, leisure facilities, sports venues, art galleries and museums, etc.
Environment: encouraged decentralisation and the use of public transport to reduce overcrowding and pollution.

6 Brittany: two thirds of France's animal products, 1000 km of coastline, has ten million tourists a

year. (The other statements describe the Auvergne.)

7 Water pollution is caused by the large number of animals in Brittany. Their manure was used as fertiliser on the fields. Rain washed the manure into rivers, which contaminated water supplies, caused algae/weeds to grow – suffocating aquatic life, and ended up in estuaries clogging fishing nets. The problem has been reduced by building water treatment plants and encouraging the farmers to farm with fewer animals.

8 Mexico/Columbia/Argentina/Chile/Brazil/ Portugal/Spain/Belgium/Italy/ Morocco/Algeria/ Poland/Turkey/Romania/Slovenia/Russia/South Korea/Malaysia

9 Advantages: cheap source of skilled labour; immigrants do the jobs that the French don't want to do; adds richness to the culture (food, fashion, music, art, etc.).
Disadvantages: ethnic tension/racism/ discrimination; unemployment/ social disadvantage; alleged drain on social services.

10 This is an answer that is too big to write in full here. The essence is that France cannot survive as a major economic power without being completely connected to the rest of the world. This includes movement of people, money, ideas, components, products, businesses, ideas, services, etc. The role of TNCs, globalisation and world trade are crucial parts of any answer.

Test your knowledge 4
Local Actions – Global Effects
1 a) Pesticide; b) roads; c) litter; d) fertilisers; e) industry; f) waste; g) leisure; h) housing; i) nitrates.

		P	E	S	T		I	C	I	D	E	S
	R	O	A	D	S							
		L	I	T		T	E	R				
F	E	R	T	I	L	I	S	E	R	S		
		I	N	D	U	S	T	R	Y			
	W	A	S	T	E							
		L	E	I	S	U	R	E				
		H	O	U	S	I	N	G				
		N	I	T	R	A	T	E	S			

2 a) true; b) false; c) true, d) false.
3 a) 1320 km; b) 185 000 km^2; c) 2200 m^3; d) 500 000; e) 1958; f) 500 000; g) 400 km.

4 Strict pollution controls; regular monitoring; rapid response to pollution; international agreements to protect the Rhine.

5

6 Limestone: permeable; formed 300 million years ago; tropical sea; soft and dissolves in rainwater. Grit stone: impermeable; formed 50 million years ago; river delta; hard and resistant to weathering.

7 Benefits: 1000 jobs, £137 m spent a year; improved infrastructure/ facilities/amenities. Problems: employment is only seasonal; overcrowding of honeypot sites; litter; footpath erosion; pollution; car parking. Solutions: National Park status; wardens, tourist information and education; footpath rebuilding; new/restored car parks.

8 Antarctica is **50** times the size of the UK. It contains two thirds of the world's **fresh water** and it plays a crucial role in managing the earth's **climate**. Only 2% of Antarctica is **rock**, the rest is **ice**. Temperatures can fall to as low as -50°C. Antarctica has a fragile **ecosystem**; affecting one part could have a disastrous effect on the whole. At the bottom of the food chain is **krill**; this tiny shrimp-like creature is vital to the survival of much larger mammals higher up the food chain, such as leopard seals and killer whales.

9 Antarctica is threatened by mining, fishing, territorial claims/conflict, tourism, global warming. Each of these points needs to be explained with more than one reason why the issue is affecting Antarctica and how it is a threat.

10 Arguments for: World Park status would ensure the continued protection of Antarctica. It would limit the impact of any of the threats above considerably. Antarctica is one of the world's last untouched wildernesses, and deserves to stay that way. It plays a crucial part in managing global climate, and the effects if this were to go wrong could be catastrophic.

Arguments against: current sources of raw materials will eventually run out and replacements are found in only a limited number of locations. Fish reserves in Antarctica are plentiful: with the world's increasing population, food sources have to be developed. People have a right to visit wilderness regions, particularly if a reason for them to be protected is their rarity and beauty. Global warming is a worldwide problem, so making Antarctica a World Park would not prevent it from being affected by global climate change.

Make sure that you include your own opinion – you could also link this issue to any of the other issues in the book, e.g. is Antarctica more important than starving people?

Answers to Practice paper

1 a) Collision
   b) Lava is sticky and slow moving because it contains silica from oceanic sediments. It can solidify in the volcano, forming a plug, pressure builds up, then the volcano explodes. When the lava flows out of the volcano it solidifies quickly, more lava solidifies on top of that, and steep sides are formed.
   c) Two from: Less preparation/less warning or monitoring/slower response and inadequate emergency services/weaker buildings and other structures. All due to lack of money/technical expertise/education/development.

2 a) 1 ½ hours.
   b) The sea draws back when a tsunami wave arrives at the coast, trough first. This gives the impression of the sea retreating.
   c) Better monitoring/early warning systems, having regular tsunami drills, having evacuation plans and shelters prepared, building sea defences at key locations.

3 a) HDI.
   b) LEDCs: Families have low incomes, so cannot afford to buy enough food. Subsistence farmers may not be able to grow enough food – poor soil/drought/disease/pests.
       MEDCs: People over-eat, because they have high incomes so are able to buy as much food as they want. Few people are farmers; they are able to buy food using global supplies. A poor crop in one country just means the crop is bought from another.

4 a) (i) A (ii) B
   b) Low cost labour. Could also be: cheap source of raw materials, large local market.
   c) Sweatshop conditions, e.g. long hours, low pay, few breaks, poor health and safety, few days off.

5 a) Disease/pests/poor weather could destroy that crop, resulting in a dramatic fall in the country's export earnings. A decline in the world price of the produce would have the same effect. Competition in that product from another country could also lead to a fall in the country's export earnings.
   b) Fair trade sells goods at a higher price, so the extra money goes to the farmers. Fair trade organisations ensure that the farmers are helped with housing, health care and education for their children.

6 a) The southern half of France is more mountainous than the northern half.
   b) Rhône.

7 a) Plotted at the 77% position on the y percentage axis.
   b) French manufacturing industry has become out of date, expensive and poorer quality than manufacturing in other countries such as China, which is more modern, cheaper and better quality.

8 a) UK and Netherlands.
   b) Brittany/Auvergne/Paris and beaches/volcanoes/Eiffel Tower (for example).

9 a) A
   b) Pass laws/regulations controlling pollution/regular monitoring of the river/building water purification plants/providing 'ladders' for salmon to use as they migrate up stream.

10 a) Carbon Dioxide.
   b) Local: ice is melting, breeding grounds are becoming unusable, icebergs and shelves are melting/breaking off.
       Global: no one knows what the effect of Antarctica melting will have on the earth's ocean and atmospheric currents.